# *BODY/TEXT IN JULIA KRISTEVA*

# BODY/TEXT IN JULIA KRISTEVA

*Religion, Women, and Psychoanalysis*

*Edited by*

## DAVID R. CROWNFIELD

STATE UNIVERSITY OF NEW YORK PRESS

Published by
State University of New York Press, Albany

© 1992   State University of New York

For information, address the State University of New York Press,
State University Plaza, Albany, NY 12246

Production by Ruth Fisher
Marketing by Theresa A. Swierzowski

**Library of Congress Cataloging-in-Publication Data**

Body/text in Julia Kristeva  :   religion, women, and psychoanalysis   /
    edited by David R. Crownfield.
        p.   cm.
    Includes bibliographical references and index.
    ISBN 0-7914-1129-X (alk. paper). —ISBN 0-7914-1130-3 (pbk.   :
alk. paper)
        1. Kristeva, Julia, 1941–   .   2. Psychoanalysis and religion.
3. Psychoanalysis and women.   4. Women and religion.
I. Crownfield, David R., 1930–   .
BF109.K69B63   1992
194—dc20
                                                                                            91-30802
10   9   8   7   6   5   4   3   2                                              CIP

# CONTENTS

Acknowledgments / vii
Pre-text / ix

**1** Situating Kristeva Differently: Psychoanalytic Readings of
Woman and Religion / 1
Diane Jonte-Pace

Inter-text 1 / 23

**2** Metaphor, Meta-Narrative, and Mater-Narrative in
Kristeva's "Stabat Mater" / 27
Marilyn Edelstein

Inter-text 2 / 53

**3** The Sublimation of Narcissism in Christian Love and Faith / 57
David R. Crownfield

Inter-text 3 / 65

**4** The Mother in Mimesis: Kristeva and Girard on
Violence and the Sacred / 67
Martha Reineke

Inter-text 4 / 87

**5** Kristeva's *Chora* and the Subject of Postmodern Ethics / 91
David Fisher

Inter-text 5 / 107

**6** Art and Religious Discourse in Aquinas and Kristeva  /  111
Cleo McNelly Kearns

Inter-text 6  /  125

**7** Joying in the Truth of Self-Division  /  129
Jean Graybeal

Inter-text 7  /  139

Extra-text: Questions  /  141

Selected Bibliography  /  145

Contributors  /  153

Index  /  155

## ( ACKNOWLEDGMENTS )

"when god lets my body be" is reprinted from TULIPS & CHIMNEYS by E. E. Cummings, Edited by George James Firmage, by permission of Liveright Publishing Corporation. Copyright 1923, 1935 and renewed 1951–1953 by E. E. Cummings. Copyright © 1973, 1976 by the Trustees for the E. E. Cummings Trust. Copyright © 1973, 1976 by George James Firmage. British Commonwealth rights by permission of HarperCollins London.

Selection from "The Poem as Icon" from "The Rock," from COLLECTED POEMS by Wallace Stevens. Copyright 1954 by Wallace Stevens. Reprinted by permission of Random House, Inc. British Commonwealth rights by permission of Faber and Faber Limited.

Selection from "But What is the Reader to Make of This" from A WAVE by John Ashbery (New York: Viking, 1984). Copyright © 1980, 1981, 1982, 1983, 1984 by John Ashbery. Reprinted by permission of Georges Borchardt, Inc.

## ( PRE-TEXT )

What follows is a set of essays; at the same time, it is an open-textured, multifocal conversation whose beginnings, ends, and boundaries are always in question. This pre-text will play the role of an introduction in several respects. First, there is a narrative of aspects of Kristeva's life and work, with some cross-reference to the sections in which we discuss her texts. This is followed by a provisional consideration of her engagement with questions of women and of feminism, and of some possible objections to her views. Next is a preview of the essays to follow, in the order of their presentation, and then in several alternative orderings and thematic groupings (in order to underscore their mutual interaction and synergy). Comments on the production of the essays and the style of their presentation then clear the way for the main course.

### 1

Julia Kristeva was born in Bulgaria in 1941. Accounts of her early years are enigmatic or inconsistent. (Leon Roudiez says, "She received her early education from French nuns. Then came the inevitable Communist Party children's groups, and, later, the party youth organizations. . . . [S]he worked on a newspaper for communist youth while pursuing literary studies at the university" (*Desire in Language* 1f). A note (n. 7) to Marilyn Edelstein's essay in this volume comments on these topics and raises some questions about Roudiez's account.) Of her religious background Kristeva herself says, "I am not a believer, but I recall having been born into a family of believers, who tried, without excessive enthusiasm, perhaps, to transmit their faith to me. . . . [In adolescence] my macabre thoughts [about faith and death] soon gave way to erotic daydreams" (*In the Beginning Was Love* 23f).

She began graduate study in Paris in 1966, the year of Jacques Lacan's *Écrits*, the year before Jacques Derrida's *Of Grammatology* and *Writing and Difference*, two years before the spontaneous and abortive revolution of French workers and students in May 1968. Her orientation to Paris was facilitated by her fellow Bulgarian, Tzvetan Todorov, who had

arrived a few years earlier. Todorov played a key role in acquainting her
with the work of the Russian discourse-theorist Mikhail Bakhtin, which
had a major part in shaping her thought.

So much of Kristeva's work responds to the agenda and the fram-
ing of the issues in Bakhtin that it may be helpful to look at a few of his
themes. Todorov has published a small book on Bakhtin, which is both
a helpful and, for Kristeva studies, a particularly appropriate source.
First of all, Bakhtin proposed to consider as the object of his analysis not
the language as a system, but the practice of discourse, especially as it
is found in texts. Much of his attention is directed to the novel, a focus
Kristeva follows.

Bakhtin held that the human subject is not an original and autonomous entity, but is constituted socially and above all by language. He
criticizes Freud because, as Todorov describes it, "Freudianism . . . conceives of the unconscious as preceding, or external to, language. Yet,
the only access we have to it is mediated by language" (Mikhail Bakhtin
31). Todorov quotes Bakhtin, in a passage that could be from Lacan except for its clarity:

> "The motifs of the unconscious revealed during psychoanalytic
> sessions by means of the method of 'free association' are *verbal re-*
> *actions* of the patient, as are all the other habitual motifs of con-
> sciousness. . . . What is reflected in these verbal utterances is not
> the dynamics of the individual soul, but the social dynamics of the
> interrelations of doctor and patient." (31)

The following passage from Bakhtin is addressed to communication theory, but its application to psychoanalysis is clear, and corresponds to Kristeva's (and Lacan's) later account:

> "In reality the relations between A and B are in a state of perma-
> nent formation and transformation; they continue to alter in the
> very process of communication. Nor is there a ready-made mes-
> sage X. It takes form in the process of communication between A
> and B. Nor is it transmitted from the first to the second, but con-
> structed between them, like an ideological bridge; it is constructed
> in the process of their interaction." (55f)

Even more Lacanian are the following: "The other is necessary to
accomplish, even if temporarily, a perception of the self. . . . The image
I see in the mirror . . . provides me with the archetype of self-percep-
tion; only someone else's gaze can give me the feeling that I form a to-

tality" (95). "There are events that, in principle, cannot unfold on the plane of a single and unified consciousness, but presuppose two consciousnesses that do not fuse; . . . whose essential and constitutive element is the relation of a consciousness to *another* consciousness, precisely because it is *other*" (99).

This last comment is written to characterize the relation between the subjectivity of the narrator and the subjectivity of the character within the structure of a novel. It is Kristeva who recognizes the homology between the Lacanian divided subject and the Bakhtinian duality in the work of fiction and makes fruitful use of it as she interweaves psychoanalytic and fictional (and religious) narratives in her explorations. Indeed, it is precisely the way in which the religious narrative reflects at the same time the multiple dynamics of fictive subjectivity and the exigencies of the desiring and suffering subject of psychoanalysis that leads Kristeva to incorporate religious materials in the discussion and that thus provides a principal gathering point for this group of essays. (Kristeva's own discussion of Bakhtin is most accessible in "Word, Dialogue, and Novel" in *Desire in Language* 64–91; reprinted in *The Kristeva Reader,* 35–61). This and other aspects of Kristeva's relation to Bakhtin are discussed in Edelstein's essay.)

While Todorov played an important role in Kristeva's entry into Paris and her engagement with Bakhtin's work, Roland Barthes (himself influenced by Bakhtin) was her principal teacher. She also did considerable work with the linguist Emile Benveniste and worked for a while as a research assistant in Claude Levi-Strauss's Laboratory of Social Anthropology. She published early essays in the radical and postmodern journal, *Tel Quel*, becoming in time one of its inner circle.

Her first book, *Sēmeiotikē*, published in 1969 in the series "Collection 'Tel Quel,' " is a collection of theoretical essays from this period, heavily influenced by Bakhtin, Barthes, and Benveniste. While it has not been translated into English, two of its essays, "The Bounded Text" and "Word, Dialogue, and Novel," are included in *Desire in Language*. Almost all the other essays in *Desire in Language* were first published in *Tel Quel*, and all were collected in her book, *Polylogue* (1977), except for a 1980 preface for the English edition. (These 1970s essays, and that preface, are the center of much of Graybeal's discussion of Kristeva.)

A trip by Kristeva and others to China in 1974 gave rise to the essay "Des Chinoises." A part of this essay dealing (for contrast) with Judaeo-Christian culture is reprinted in *The Kristeva Reader.* It makes substantive observations on Biblical monotheism and Christian idealization of virginity, which none of us have elected to discuss in the present volume. She married Philippe Sollers (the subject of "The Novel As Polylogue" in *Desire in Language*); the birth of their son in 1976 appears to provide a personal background for her essay, "Stabat Mater" (but see Edelstein's essay for some reservations on its autobiographical status).

Kristeva's early work is heavy with theory, bringing Marxist, psychoanalytic, and Bakhtinian/Barthian perspectives to bear on central issues concerning the nature of discourse and the novel, and focusing increasingly on the dynamic interplay between the formal, public system of language (what Lacan calls the symbolic) and somatic, rhythmic, emotional functions that operate with their own logic and appear to have their roots in the preverbal stages of child development. Lacan, at this stage, recognizes only the imaginary register in which the child's identity is constituted by the mirror image, by the regard of the other, and the world is marked by iconic images rather than signifying signs. Kristeva, however, finds here a complex semiotics of tactile and kinesthetic differences, inscribed in a primordial *chora* (receptive space: Plato's term, from the *Timaeus*), that founds the experiential territory of the somatic dyad of mother and child. (David Fisher's essay gives central attention to the significance, for the question of ethics, of this conception of the *chora* and the semiotic register, especially as she developed it in her 1974 dissertation, of which the theoretical sections appear in English as *Revolution in Poetic Language*.)

The exploration of the semiotics of the *chora* led Kristeva to avant-garde literature, to the psychology of psychotic and borderline states, and to the dynamics of infancy. In all of these areas, the interpersonal construction of meaning Bakhtin had emphasized plays a crucial role, and the function of transference and counter-transference becomes critical. This, together with frustration with the abstract impersonality of literary theory and a disillusionment with then-current politics, led her to undergo and to qualify to practice psychoanalysis.

In an interview in *Partisan Review* in 1986, Kristeva says that Jacques Lacan was not only an intellectual influence but a friend, and that for those reasons and others she was *not* analyzed by Lacan, as is widely supposed (even the American dust jacket of her *Black Sun* says she was). In addition to the personal and intellectual relationship, she says, there was the fact that the Lacanians were very much politicized around their role in the psychoanalytic movement and around other issues of power. She also holds that a heterogeneity (plurality) of approach is essential in the clinical work of psychoanalysis. So hers was not a Lacanian, but a more mainstream analysis. Lacan's intellectual influence on her work is evident, but it is not initially or essentially brought into play through her experience and training in psychoanalysis. Rather, it preceded her analysis and was modified by it.

Lacan's importance depends largely on his recognition of the structural analogue between the theory of signification in Saussure and his followers in structural linguistics and the account of signification of dream-elements in Freud's *The Interpretation of Dreams*. For both Saussure and Freud, signs (dream-symbols) are a composite of a sensory signifier and a signified meaning; the relation of signifier and signified is arbitrary (idiosyncratic, in the dream); the structural relations, differences, oppositions among signifiers—rather than any inherent value of individual ones—is the basis of their achievement of effects of meaning. In Lacan, this extends beyond the dream to the symptom; and, conversely, the overdetermination of signifiers by the dynamics of desire is generalized by Lacan from Freud back into linguistics.

As a result, Lacan develops a distinctive psychoanalytic theory of the relation between the acquisition of language and the dynamics of personal development. Blocked by the father (not by any behavior of the father, but by the function, the position, the very existence of the role of the father) from total possession of mother's desire, the child is forced to substitute other gratifications, other objects of desire, other roles to play or places to play them. This positional logic of substitution, of representing one thing by another, of displacing desire along a chain of representatives, is the foundation of the formal order of language, of what Lacan calls the symbolic order. Because of its origin in the displacement imposed by the paternal function, Lacan also calls this order the Law of the Father or the Name (*Nom*, homophonic with *non*, "no") of the Father.

In Lacan's theory, the infant begins in an incoherent plurality of sensations. At some point between six and eighteen months, the child sees itself in a mirror, or is mirrored to itself in the regard of the parent. This reflection provides an image of unity with which the child comes to identify. It is this imaginary self that is the foundation of the ego and that is signified in language once the symbolic order is in play. Thus, behind and beneath the symbolic order lies the imaginary order, characterized essentially by a self identified and unified by its reflection from the other and by iconic, nonsignifying modes of representation of the world. The interplay between the substitutionary unreality of the symbolic and the mirroring unreality of the imaginary, both always struggling against the exigency of the real—somatic intensity, as ecstasy and as pain; need; the inaccessible Other; death—, constitutes the dynamics of life and of suffering. ("Real," for Lacan and Kristeva, indicates the insistent, inescapable, heterogeneous; "reality" ordinarily suggests that which conforms to a consensual discourse about what is real. These issues are further elaborated and refined in Kearns's essay.)

Kristeva largely accepts this Lacanian analysis but modifies it through a more extensive analysis of pre-Oedipal dynamics. Rather than an initial state of fragmentation, she begins from an emergent differentiation within the somatic unity of mother and child. (In "Stabat Mater" she considers this emergence from the maternal point of view; Edelstein gives it substantial discussion. Other Kristevan texts center attention on the infant and the "zero degree of subjectivity," as she calls it in *Tales of Love*, which Crownfield and Reineke examine in detail.) All subsequent experience is inscribed in this original pre-space, ur-container, *chora*, and constitutes a bodily semiotics that serves as the foundation for the possibility of the symbolic structures of language. Kristeva thus speaks of the semiotic order, in this sense of a somatic semiotics before the emergence of the Oedipal and symbolic.

Kristeva's psychoanalysis and training extended approximately from 1976 to 1979, and she has since practiced psychoanalysis in Paris, as well as teaching in the Department of Texts and Documents of the University of Paris VII and periodically in comparative literature at Columbia University. Her major writings of this later period, *Powers of Horror* (1980), *Tales of Love* (1983), *In the Beginning Was Love: Psychoanalysis and Faith* (1985), *Black Sun* (1987), and *Étrangers à nous-même* (1989), are more relaxed, more readable, more concrete, more plural—some would say, more human — than the more theoretical works of the late 1960s and the 1970s, though the basic conceptual structure remains. In each case, she explores in the Western tradition religious and literary images of human being, with respect to issues successively of abjection, narcissism, and love, faith, depression, and estrangement (and foreignness — the French word *étranger* says both "stranger" and "foreigner" at once). Many of the themes of these works will be discussed in the essays that follow, though except for this introduction we have not commented on *Étrangers*, and only Jonte-Pace's essay deals with *Black Sun*.

2

Throughout this history, Kristeva has been engaged with the questions of being a woman, of roles of women in the past, present, and future, of the status of gender in theory and practice. She writes consciously as a woman, but with reservations about the specific agendas of contemporary feminisms and of *l'écriture féminine*, the French "feminine writing" of her contemporaries such as Luce Irigaray and Helene Cixous, with whom she is occasionally and inexactly classified. A number of the themes and issues she raises in regard to these matters are discussed in the following essays. Edelstein takes up specifically some contemporary criticisms of Kristeva's relation to feminism; Jonte-Pace also gives substantive attention to her contributions to and criticisms of feminism, though not to her critics. Graybeal also discusses Kristeva's likening of certain feminisms to a religion, in "Women's Time" and "Woman Can Not Be Defined."

Kristeva engages directly with what may be the most radical predicament that confronts the very project of a feminist discourse. Lacan characterized the symbolic, the public realm of language and discourse in its logical, syntactical, semantic functions, as the Law of the Father, the substitutive trace and representative of the defeat of the child's Oedipal desire, the concealed and indirect persistence of the phallus, the marker of what mother wants (is imagined to want). If cognitive discourse is, then, paternal, male, phallic, how is feminine discourse to proceed? Is it necessary to submit to paternal and masculine authority in order to communicate? Or is it possible to devise a non logical semiotics of the imaginary, of music and dance and play, sufficient to enable a full feminine being and expression and effective sociality without the negativity of the masculine language? (Graybeal's essay opens some of these latter possibilities.)

Kristeva sees exclusive reliance on either option as a mistake. She thus distances herself on the one hand from a sort of political feminism that wants to take over the linguistic means of production and achieve a feminine mastery, and on the other from a cultic and mythic feminism that abandons the rigor of cognitive discourse. She does not offer a totalist program to solve the problem but favors situational subversion, disruption, and displacement of cognitive discourse, while at the same time relying almost exclusively on that discourse in almost all her own work. (The extent to which "Stabat Mater," with its two-column text, is an exception is considered in Edelstein's essay; Jonte-Pace also touches on it.)

Kristeva prefers to engage the conflict of phallic language and feminine discourse at another level. Lacan recognized, more explicitly and consistently than Freud, that the primary parent for all children is the mother and that father is the third party who displaces the child from centrality. (In his view, it is the girl's — learned — strategy of managing this displacement through identification with mother and the boy's through substitution of an other for mother that is the basis of gender difference [Écrits: A Selection 146ff].) Mother and father are thus not natural archetypes of female and male identity but parental roles that function initially in the same way for all of us. Language disposes of gender difference through correlation of gender names with the presence and absence of the penis. Kristeva makes a double move behind the Oedipal triangle on which Lacan, like Freud, is fixed. On the one hand, she develops the centrality of the archaic maternal function, the *chora*, the semiotics of the flesh. With respect to the paternal character of language, this plays out as the recognition of the constant codetermination of discourse by the archaic semiotics as well as the formal symbolics—a codetermination operative for all of us, only (falsely) suppressed in patriarchal domination.

At the same time, Kristeva brings the father back into this prehistory. Not a gendered, genitally specific male figure, but the third party, Mother's Other, for whom the child is object of discourse and of regard, and in mimicry of whom the child begins to be a subject. In some sense, then, having moved back into what had been regarded as exclusively maternal territory, she betrays it to the enemy by bringing the third party into the primordial situation. But it is crucial to see here that it is not the function of the *masculine* but the function of the *other,* the *third*, that is decisive. This argument is, indeed, central to her late work because it is in the triadic foundation of subjectivity that there lies the possibility of effective sociality, of the effective sublimation of narcissism. (Crownfield and Reineke have organized their essays around this structure, which also functions for Kearns.)

One key aspect of Kristeva's resistance to programmatic feminism may be indicated by a brief reference to *Strangers to Ourselves*. The book deals with the problem of the stranger, the outsider, the foreigner — with explicit recognition of the contemporary French political conflict about the status of foreign workers. She is interested in the origins, the dynamics, the provenance of the idea of the stranger, including its function in constituting the political community. And she finds, as the title indicates, that the problem of the stranger is internal to each of us. This theme relates to those found in her analysis of abjection in *Powers of Horror,* where the abhorrent, the intolerable and absolutely-to-be-excluded, is a representative of a problematic separation of self from mother, and thus of the terrifying threat of otherness to one who is uncertain of one's own boundary. (The maternal matrix of this structure is responsible for the general tendency to target women for abjection and scapegoating, as Reineke argues; Jonte-Pace and Graybeal also comment on this problematic).

3

Only less controversial than Kristeva's relation to feminism is her increasingly appreciative consideration of religion. While she shares the contemporary intellectual consensus that the era of religion is past, she recognizes in its semiotic/symbolic structures images of the split self, of desire, of narcissism and its sublimation, of abjection, of paternal and maternal functions, that have been of great force in the Western textual tradition and that resonate strongly with the imagery through which her psychoanalytic subjects articulate their pain and their desire for love. These issues arise throughout her work, and the role of religious discourse in articulating them has been of central importance in her writings of the 1980s. It is these questions that have gathered this collection of essays.

We begin with an essay by Diane Jonte-Pace, who notes that psychoanalysis from Freud to Winnicott to Lacan has associated religion with femininity and illusion, though on different grounds and with different valuations. Kristeva continues this connection, in several texts the analysis of which enables Jonte-Pace to uncover a deeper association between the feminine and otherness and ultimately death. Marilyn Edelstein moves the focus from the question of woman to the figure of mother, in an analysis of the essay, "Stabat Mater," which focuses a discussion of various of Kristeva's critics as well as leading into questions of the status of the author and the practice of reading.

David Crownfield summarizes Kristeva's account of narcissism and the triadic foundation of subjectivity and her use of this structure to explicate the force and limits of Christianity. The essay closes with the question whether psychoanalytic thought participates in the same illusory and fictive character as Christianity, and it leaves open a space for their continued conversation. Martha Reineke begins with the same triadic structure, in the somewhat different form in which it is presented in Rene Girard's analyses of violence and the sacred. Reineke goes on to argue that Kristeva's gendered account of the originary (infantile) triad provides a sounder foundation than Girard's and makes evident the grounds for the characteristic choice of women as sacrificial victims and scapegoats. David Fisher takes the same foundation in another direction, into the divided nature of the ethical subject and the extent to which an internal heteronomy of the archaic maternal body-space is at the center of that division.

Crownfield's, Reineke's, and Fisher's essays all combine theoretical analysis with aspects of the application of Kristeva's work to specific topics: the semiotic efficacy of Christian theology, the sacrificial foundation of social existence, and the internal heteronomy in the ethical subject, respectively. While not without theoretical interest, the last two essays focus more definitely on the side of applications. Cleo Kearns considers the role of imagination in Kristeva and Thomas Aquinas from the point of view of the function of religious discourse in practice, and

specifically in prayer. Jean Graybeal concludes the collection with reflections on *jouissance* as the play of the split subject, and on religious
phenomena (especially Vodou) in which this play is enacted.

If the reader of this volume would like to structure the reading of
the essays around the chronological development of Kristeva's work,
the best place to begin would be with Fisher's discussion of the *chora*,
our most intensive examination of *Revolution in Poetic Language* (1974).
Graybeal works primarily with essays from the period 1974–80, including those in *Desire in Language* (1980) and "Women's Time" (1979). Edelstein focuses on "Stabat Mater" (1976), with a wide range of references
to work before and after. Kearns uses some of these same materials,
plus *Tales of Love* (1983). The most focused examination of *Powers of Horror* is in Reineke's essay, which also develops the theory of narcissism in
*Tales of Love*. Crownfield centers on *Tales of Love* and *In the Beginning Was
Love* (1985). Jonte-Pace also deals with "Stabat Mater," "Women's
Time," *Powers of Horror,* and *In the Beginning;* I list her last only because
she is the only one who discusses *Black Sun* (1987). Except for the paragraph in this introduction, none of us has engaged with *Étrangers à nous-
même* (1989).

In situating Kristeva in relation to other figures, one might begin,
as we do, with Jonte-Pace's discussion of Freud, Winnicott and Lacan
on the relation of "woman" and "religion." Reineke gives systematic attention to the relation between the work of Kristeva and that of Rene
Girard with respect to violence, sacrifice, identity, and the foundations
of social existence. The feminist criticisms (especially with regard to the
category of motherhood) are considered most directly in Edelstein's essay. Edelstein and Kearns consider aspects of Kristeva's relation to contemporary literary theory. In Kearns, Thomas Aquinas's theory of
imagination comes into play; in Fisher, questions of Aristotle and Hegel
as well as contemporary philosophical and Christian ethicists; in Graybeal, reflections on Vodou as it might illuminate some of the Kristevan
issues.

Conceptually, the *chora* and the notion of the semiotic are given
most attention by Fisher. The question of woman is an organizing
theme for Jonte-Pace, Reineke, and Edelstein and plays a decisive role
for Kearns as well. (It is necessarily part of the discussion for all of us
and throughout.) Edelstein's discussion of "Stabat Mater" and Fisher's
consideration of Kristeva's relevance for postmodern ethics are the only
essays in which her understanding of religion is not an organizing
theme. (In Reineke, to be more precise, it is Kristeva's analyses of abjection and narcissism, as a corrective to Girard's understanding of religion, that is thematized.) Abjection gets substantive attention in Jonte-

Pace as well as Reineke. The question of ethics comes into play in Edelstein as well as in Fisher; in so far as Reineke's analysis centers on the constitutive role of abjection in establishing community, her work also bears on the matter of ethics. Narcissism is decisive for Reineke and Crownfield. Illusion is important for Jonte-Pace, Graybeal, and Crownfield. Crownfield gives central attention to her analyses of Christianity.

The problem of language is inseparable from discussions of Kristeva. The maternal matrix of the semiotic is in Fisher's eye, and the notion of a signifying practice is the link to ethics in his reading. Text and reading are pivotal for Edelstein; absence and difference for Jonte-Pace. The decisive role(s) of art for Kristeva, especially as alternative to religion, is in play especially in Kearns, but also in Edelstein.

None of these authors is a psychoanalyst, and the essays are not oriented to technical psychoanalytic issues. But it would be impossible to discuss Kristeva without extensive engagement with psychoanalytic themes. The general questions of psychoanalytic interpretations of "woman," and of religion (including illusion and wish fulfilment), are engaged throughout; Jonte-Pace gives them most attention, with consideration of parallels between Freud, Winnicott, Lacan, and Kristeva in their treatment of these two issues. (Judith Van Herik's discussion of Freud is much in play in all this). Crownfield and Reineke give some detailed examination to the etiology and structure of narcissism, including the Kristevan focus on a pre-Oedipal family triangle. Narcissism and other pre-Oedipal issues are also engaged in Fisher, who especially attends to the maternal *chora*. Questions of the phallus, castration, penis envy, are discussed in Jonte-Pace, Edelstein, and Crownfield. Reineke gives major play to topics from *Totem and Taboo*, especially as treated by Rene Girard: violence, incest, incorporation, dismemberment. Jonte-Pace discusses the death drive and the *fort-da* game; Crownfield, transference, sublimation, and analytic treatment; Reineke, identification. The Lacanian distinction of imaginary, symbolic, and real (and Kristeva's semiotic/symbolic pair), and the correlation of the symbolic with castration, are important for Edelstein, Crownfield, Fisher, and Graybeal. *Jouissance* is central for Graybeal and important in Jonte-Pace. Abjection functions significantly in Jonte-Pace, Reineke, and Fisher, and the true-real in Kearns.

4

Four of these essays, in earlier form, were presented together in a session of the American Academy of Religion in Anaheim in 1989; Fisher's and Kearns's essays were originally presented at other sessions of that same annual meeting of the academy. Correspondence and conversations, and reading of one another's work, have made more of a cooperative effort of it than is the case in most such collections. While time limitations have precluded making the commentaries on the essays formally collective, I have benefited by the collective spirit of the work thoughout and have tried to make it as much as possible a conversation among the essayists, rather than just with me.

To reflect this conversational dimension and to underscore the polyfocal, open-textured, synergetic character of the work, brief commentaries are inserted between the essays. These inter-texts are directed primarily to highlighting the questions the essays raise for one another, with occasional recognition of an interplay with other authors whose work questions and is questioned by our essays. In lieu of a "conclusion" — a closure — we exit with an Extra-text, a focusing of questions still open, directions in which the conversation must continue beyond the covers of the book. This strategy has posed some problems for my role as both editor and one of seven authors. I have tried to maintain a consistent separation of voice, referring to the Crownfield essay in the third person except in direct response to it, and restraining the assertion of author-ity as editor. If this produces the effect of a split subject, that is in keeping with our subject matter.

One of my co-workers merits individual comment. Martha Reineke appears in this volume formally only as one of seven authors. But she has been an invaluable consultant and conversation partner throughout, in the development of the project, in the selection and interpretation of the essays, in the development of my own contribution. She has drawn my attention to essays I would have missed, she has asked questions and made observations that have opened many doors for me. Above all, she has spent hours helping me struggle with the texts on Kristeva's theory of narcissism, without which my own essay could not have been written. It is merely because she needed to protect her time for her own work that she is not a full co-editor.

# SITUATING KRISTEVA DIFFERENTLY:
## Psychoanalytic Readings of Woman and Religion*

**Diane Jonte-Pace**

*Diane Jonte-Pace begins our collection with an essay directly on our title theme: religion, women, and psychoanalysis. She keys on a structural parallel in the relations among these three ideas in Freud, D. W. Winnicott, and Jacques Lacan and proceeds to Kristeva's radically different but still structurally comparable consideration of the triad. In conclusion, she proposes a strong thesis as to the grounds and consequences of this persistent homology.*

### PART I: WOMAN AND RELIGION

If the unanswerable question for an earlier decade was Freud's "What do women want?" the comparable question in today's conversations is surely "What does 'woman' mean?" Alice Jardine points out that "it has become increasingly difficult to find a major theoretician . . . who is not concerned in one way or another with 'woman' " (1985, 34). "Woman" has come to be a metaphor for otherness, for marginality, for writing, for the demise of the autonomous subject, for the unconscious, for God, and for the unrepresentable.

"What *does* 'woman' mean?" — Julia Kristeva poses the question and defers the answer—as does Jacques Lacan. For Lacan, "nothing can be said of woman" (1982, 152): "there is no such thing as The Woman. . . . There is 'woman' only as excluded by the nature of things which is the nature of words" (144). Kristeva accepts this Lacanian tenet: "Indeed, she (woman) does not exist with a capital W, possessor of some mythical unity" ("Women's Time" 1986, 205). But for Kristeva, while marginalized, woman is not wholly negated: "I understand by

1

'woman,' " she says, "that which cannot be represented, something that is not said, something above and beyond nomenclatures and ideologies" (Marks 1981, 137).

These contemporary articulations of the meaning of woman differ widely from earlier psychoanalytic formulations: though Freud despaired of knowing what women want, he did have a sense of what woman means, as did his British follower D. W. Winnicott. For Freud, woman, as mother, is object of the son's desire; as daughter, she is the recipient of paternal consolation. Winnicott's woman is primarily the "good enough mother," a mirror for the infant's developing subjectivity.

Although the meaning of woman differs substantially for these psychoanalytic theorists, the differences in their analyses conceal a set of common structural assumptions regarding woman. This set of assumptions involves a homology of woman and religion: in spite of radically different understandings of woman, these theorists "engender religion" as feminine. I am particularly interested in Julia Kristeva's multiple linkages of woman and religion, but I want to situate Kristeva's analysis within the context of other psychoanalytic readings of the meaning of woman and the meaning of religion. Although some have argued that we must read Kristeva outside the limits of psychoanalytic beliefs, practices and programs, I maintain that Kristeva is best understood when read in the context of psychoanalysis. Thus, I will examine Freud's *renunciation of faith and the feminine,* Winnicott's *recovery of faith and the feminine,* and Lacan's move *beyond faith and the feminine* as the context for a discussion of Kristeva's complex analysis of these terms. The homology I'm tracing in Kristeva and in these three other psychoanalytic theorists allows a degree of slippage: if woman slides into "the feminine" and "maternality," religion slips toward God, the believer, the sacred, and faith.

Having established a homology of woman and religion in psychoanalytic theory in part I of this paper, I will briefly consider, in part II, the question of why these terms are homologized. I will argue that the discourses of gender and religion both articulate a concern with absence. It is absence, formulated as non-being in the discourse of religion, and formulated as difference or female lack in the discourse of gender, that underlies the homology of woman and religion. These investigations of woman and religion, absence and difference, will lead to some concluding remarks about the potential of psychoanalytic theory to critique misogyny by revealing the structures linking the fear of woman with the fear of death.

*Freud: Renunciation of Faith and the Feminine*

Freud links both religion and femininity to developmental inferiority and illusion. His analysis is based on a metaphor of cultural and psychological evolution: with individual/developmental progress and cultural/evolutionary progress, he argues, the "feminine" illlusion of religion will be renounced in favor of "masculine" rationality. Superimposed on this evolutionary schema in Freud's writings is a view of dependence and autonomy in which dependence is logically linked with religion and the feminine, and autonomy with reason and masculinity.

While some of his early work on religion focuses on ritual and other texts center on God imagery, morality, and mysticism, Freud's primary definition for religion is *belief:* consolatory belief, belief that God exists, belief in eternal life. The belief in a divine caring father, according to Freud, is an illusory belief, i e., a wish fulfillment. Illusions, including the illusion of religion, are not necessarily wrong, false, or delusory; rather, Freud argues in *Future of an Illusion,* they are *unprovable* and they *originate in unconscious wishes.* But religious illusions are dangerous because they keep us in infantile relationships of dependence to a deity whose existence is unprovable. Dependence is equivalent to immaturity, while autonomy is equivalent to maturity. Freud characterized psychological, intellectual, and moral maturity as the renunciation of attachments, dependencies, and illusions. He glowingly described "the resignation of the human being who submits himself to *Ananke* (necessity), to the laws of nature, and who expects no alleviation from the goodness or grace of God" ("Leonardo da Vinci and a Memory of his Childhood" 124 – 125). Thus for Freud, psychological dependence on a comforting parental figure, whether the human parent or the divine father, constitutes immaturity. It is something to be outgrown and renounced.

This entire nexus of terms is gendered: the oedipal family is the reigning metaphor. The pre-Oedipal child lives in a dependent and illusory world: comforting parents foster the illusion of a comforting universe. For the male child, incestuous desires for the mother, Oedipal conflicts with the father, and the emergence of castration anxiety serve to dislodge these structures. Through a successful resolution of the Oedipal conflict, the male child gains the skills that he can later translate into the renunciation of libidinal wishes, unconsciously motivated illusions, and dependence. Ideally, he will achieve an acceptance of socially sanctioned, superego morality, and a resigned, observant reality

orientation, always on the alert for hidden wishes underlying thoughts
— a position of masculine, postreligious rationality and renunciative
morality.

And what of the daughter in this Oedipal family? The Oedipal
conflict is not fully engaged. The daughter's love of the mother poses no
threat to the Oedipal father, and without male genitals, castration anxiety cannot emerge in the girl. Without a full blown Oedipal crisis the
resolution of Oedipal conflict and all its cultural concomitants are impossible. The daughter is doomed to remain in a dependent relationship with the father and will be capable neither of reason nor of full renunciation of libido, dependence, illusion, or faith. In the Freudian
psychic economy, Van Herik points out, the "qualities of the . . . believer, the feminine man, or the woman are the same: a weak superego,
a poorly developed sense of morality, a restricted intellect, opposition
to cultural advance, insufficient respect for reality, *Ananke* and *Logos*"
(1982, 192). Thus for Freud, the homology of woman and religion is
based on a linkage of daughters and religious believers. Believers are
like daughters; gods are like fathers; and sons are like nonbelievers.

*Winnicott: Reclaiming Faith and the Feminine*

If Freud links religion with fathers and daughters, Winnicott associates
it instead with mothers and children. Psychoanalytic object relations
theorist and pediatrician D. W. Winnicott has been acclaimed for enact-
ing a radical shift in psychoanalytic thinking about the meaning of the
human subject, of gender, and of religion. Winnicott replaces Freud's
drive theory of human motivation with a conceptual framework in
which relations with others constitute the fundamental building blocks
of mental life. He challenges the centrality of the Oedipal conflict and
castration complex in psychological and cultural development, positing
instead that the period during which the maternal-infant relationship
predominates is the crucial context out of which the self is constituted.
Thus he rescues the pre-Oedipal mother from the "dark continent" to
which Freud exiled her. The mother in Winnicott's theory is more than
the object of incestuous desire—as good enough mother, "the one who
makes active adaptation to the infant's needs" (1971, 10), she is an active
subject, a primary architect of the human psyche. In addition, Winnicott challenges Freud's understanding of autonomous maturity and renunciation of wishes as the psychological ideal, arguing that dependence is not merely an early developmental stage to be outgrown, but
that there are mature forms of dependence and interdependence.

In effect, Winnicott reverses the structural arrangements of Freud's evaluation of gender and religion but retains the homology of woman and religion. God becomes maternal rather than paternal, and while religious belief remains "illusory," illusion is reclaimed as normative, creative, and epistemologically legitimate. Winnicott locates the capacity for illusion in an early phase of perceptual and emotional development and argues that illusion need not be false. Illusion is simultaneously real and projected; it is a central component of perception and of knowing in general. Perception is a dual process of creation of the other from within and discovery of the other from without. Unlike Freud, Winnicott does not see illusion as something immature to be renounced; rather, it is an inevitable part of knowing and it is highly valued: it "is retained in the intense experiencing that belongs to the arts and to religion and to imaginative living and to creative scientific work" (1971, 14).

For Winnicott the realm of illusion is deeply linked with early maternal care rather than with paternal protection and consolation. "The realm of illusion . . . is at the basis of initiation of experience. This early stage in development is made possible by the mother's special capacity for making adaptation to the needs of her infant, thus allowing the infant the illusion that what the infant creates really exists" (14). Thus the creation/discovery of the psyche and the creation/discovery of the phenomena of culture, including religion, emerge from this pre-Oedipal phase of maternal-infant relationship. By linking culture and mother, rather than insisting that only the Oedipal father can create culture, Winnicott inverts the central terms of Freud's equation.

Thus mothers, daughters, religious belief, and illusion are redefined and religion is reclaimed. Freud's critiques of religion, the feminine, and dependence are reversed in an object-relational recovery of faith and the feminine. The negative evaluation of the feminine and religion becomes a positive evaluation, yet all the pieces of the argument stay in place: the homology of woman and religious belief remains intact. (For a more complete discussion of Winnicott and religion, see Jonte-Pace 1985, 1987. For the differential effects of early object relations on daughters and on sons, see Chodorow 1978).

*Lacan: Beyond God and Woman*

Unlike Winnicott, Jacques Lacan does not intend to reclaim religion or gender from Freud's critique. Instead both categories are thrown into question in an attack on all "universals," "humanisms," or "truths." In fact, Lacan is a vituperative critic of object relations theory, crusading against what he sees as its misrepresentation of Freud: its overemphasis on the mother, its abandonment of the questions of gender differentiation and castration anxiety, its false constructions of merger and nonfragmented subjectivity, its humanistic belief in a unified self, and its repression of the "phallic" in culture. (See Rose 1982, Mitchell 1982, Butler 1990, Frosh 1987.) Yet Lacan maintains the Freudian and Winnicottian congruence of femininity and religion by associating woman with God even while denying the ontological reality of both.

Lacan's lectures "God and the *Jouissance* of The Woman" and "A Love Letter" in his Seminar XX "Encore," are the site of his most sustained discussions of 'woman.' Here he explicitly "takes up what Freud left aside . . . the 'What does woman want?' " (1982, 151; see also 1981, 28). He claims, as noted above, "there is no such thing as The woman, where the definite article stands for the universal. There is no such thing as The woman since of her essence . . . she is not all . . . There is woman only as excluded by the nature of things which is the nature of words" (1982, 144). Woman is thus always outside of discourse and cannot be represented. While the representationality or referentiality of language itself is called into question in Lacan's work, "woman" is doubly barred from the "symbolic," phallocentric realm of linguistic discourse.

Lacan proceeds to link woman with God, religion, mysticism, and the soul through an illumination of alterity and *"jouissance"* (Lacan's term for sexual or spiritual ecstasy). Woman has a supplementary *jouissance* "beyond the phallus," he states (145). This *jouissance* is also attained by those, male *and* female, who "sense that there must be a *jouissance* which goes beyond. That is what we call a mystic" (147). Though "nothing can be said of the woman" (152), she is "of the order of the infinite" and is homologized with God through her otherness: "the unmoved mover, the supreme being . . . is situated in the place, the opaque place of the *jouissance* of the Other—that Other which if she existed the woman might be. It is in so far as her *jouissance* is radically Other that the woman has a (greater) relation to God" (153).

Lacan is *not* making a mystical or romantic claim that woman and God are ineffable but real. Rather, the alterity or irreducible Otherness of God/woman place both outside of language. For Lacan there is no prediscursive reality, "no feminine outside language . . . the feminine is constituted as a division in language, a division which produces the feminine as its negative term. If woman is defined as Other it is because the definition produces her as other, and not because she has another essence" (Rose 1982, 55). If, as we have seen, Freud makes illusion a wish fulfillment that is not necessarily in contradistinction to reality, and Winnicott makes illusion a necessary component of reality, Lacan reverses Winnicott's project, in effect, making reality a dimension of illusion. The "Real" for Lacan is not reality, and our perceptions of "reality" are socially and linguistically constructed "fictions."

Lacan links "woman" with the notion of the immortal soul through a kind of inverse relationship: "For the soul to come into being, she, the woman, is differentiated from it, and this has always been the case. Called woman (dit-femme) and defamed (difamme). The most famous things that have been handed down in history have been strictly speaking the most defamatory that could be said of them" (Lacan 1982, 156). Women's denigration, in other words, is the precondition for man's belief in his own soul and in eternal life. Misogyny and denial of death thus are linked, a point to which we shall return.

Thus even with Lacan's radically new definition of the key terms we find that God and woman are homologous. Lacan's linkage of God and woman is even more dramatic and explicit than Freud's and Winnicott's. What was for Freud and Winnicott a structural pattern, embedded in the texts but not immediately apparent, became overt in Lacan. This homology is central to Julia Kristeva's texts as well, often as an explicit thesis.

### Kristeva: Word Meets Flesh

Kristeva offers a complex analysis of religion and woman that embraces but moves beyond Lacan's formulations. As noted above, Kristeva hesitates before the task of defining woman: "Woman can never be defined ... a woman cannot be" (1981, 137). Nevertheless, she explores the discourses of motherhood in Western religion in an attempt to articulate something of the meaning of woman. She asks, "If it is not possible to say of a woman what she is (without running the risk of abolishing her difference), would it perhaps be different concerning the mother, since that is the only function of 'the other sex' to which we can definitely attribute existence?" (1986, 161).

Though there are many sites in Kristeva's work illuminating the homology of woman and religion, I want to comment primarily on four representative texts: "Stabat Mater," "Women's Time," *Powers of Horror,* and *In the Beginning Was Love* (see also, for example, *Tales of Love, Desire in Language* and *Black Sun*). "Stabat Mater" describes the splitting or di-

vision of woman in theological discourse, and thus might be seen as a
critique of sexism of Western religions. However, it is not an indictment
of Christianity—rather it explores the power and meaning of the image
of the Virgin Mary and seems to urge a new ethic, an "heretical ethic"
or "heréthique" drawn from the rich tradition of Christian Mariology.
"Women's Time" and *Powers of Horror* represent Kristeva's explorations
of the religious dimensions of the negativity of woman: the danger-
ously ideological aspects of radical feminism and the polluting, "abject"
aspects of the maternal. *In the Beginning* represents an examination of a
more benign side of the feminine, uncovering the source of religious
faith and psychoanalytic healing in maternal love.

The title of Kristeva's essay "Stabat Mater" (1977, trans. 1986) refers to the Latin hymn on the sorrow of the Virgin Mary at the Crucifixion. The text intertwines two narratives in parallel columns: on the left
is a series of lyrical reflections on pregnancy, childbirth, and relation
with a son. One assumes this is a personal or autobiographical account:
the mother's discourse on motherhood. On the right is a discussion of
the history of the cult of the Virgin Mary drawing in part upon the writings of the Fathers of the Church—the father's discourse on motherhood. Kristeva creates a tightly woven tapestry from the interplay of the
mother's and the fathers' words on the maternal. On the left, in bold-
face type, "my body," "my newborn," "my flesh," laughter, tears, pain,
smells, and sounds evoke the Kristevan prelinguistic, affect-laden "semiotic" realm, while on the right, set apart by neat margins, Augustine,
Bernard of Clairvaux, Chrysostom, Dante, and Freud, articulate the
Kristevan and Lacanian "symbolic," the realm of language and meaningful discourse for the speaking subject. But the two texts cannot be
sharply divided. Although the fathers speak on the right, the voice is
Kristeva's: the mother/writer appropriates the words of the fathers
about the mother. And although the styles contrast dramatically, a
number of common themes are present in both, including two that are
especially significant for our purposes: the splitting or division in the
meaning of woman in the texts of Christianity and the relation of the
mother to the origins of religious belief.

The splitting of the mother is described in this split text—the body
of the text mirrors the body of the mother. The "mother's" experiential
text reads: "there is this other abyss that opens up between the body
and what had been its inside; there is the abyss between the mother and
the child . . . the child, whether he or she, is irremediably an other . . . a
mother is a continuous separation, a division of the very flesh. And consequently a division of language—and it has always been so" (178). The

"father's" discursive text echoes the "mother's," presenting Marian theology as a dramatic splitting of the woman: maternal generativity is split from sin, from sex, and from death. As if to underscore a deeper association of mothers with death, Marian theology inverts this connection making Mary "alone of all her sex" the mother who does not die. Maternal generativity, sexuality, and death are torn asunder. In the reduplicated "division of the very flesh" of the mother's body, the splitting of the Madonna into virgin and mother, and the division of the text itself, word meets flesh.

Kristeva does not lack appreciation for the efficacy of the cult of Mary, which, she believes, has provided powerful symbolism for female identity: the cult of Mary "was able to attract women's wishes for identification. . . . The virginal maternal is a way (not among the less effective ones) of dealing with feminine paranoia" (180). If the Virgin Mary once provided a unified vision of meaning, ethics, and aesthetics for women, Kristeva's text raises troubling questions about the contemporary period: "motherhood . . . today remains, after the Virgin, without a discourse" (184). Again emphasizing the linkage of motherhood with death/non-death in the cult of Mary, she urges a search for a new, feminine, ethic: "For an heretical ethics, separated from morality, an her-ethics, is perhaps no more than that which in life makes bonds, thoughts, and therefore the thought of death bearable. Herethics is undeath [a-mort], love . . . Eia Mater, fons amoris. So let us again listen to the *Stabat Mater* and the music, all the music" (185).

Also prominent in this text is Kristeva's exploration of the relation of the mother to God and to religious belief. "Every God," says Kristeva, "even including the God of the Word, relies on a mother Goddess. Christianity is perhaps also the last of the religions to have displayed in broad daylight the bipolar structure of belief: on the one hand, the difficult experience of the Word . . . on the other, the reassuring wrapping in the proverbial mirage of the mother" (176). In asserting that 'In the beginning was the Word,' she suggests, "Christians must have found such a postulate sufficiently hard to believe [that] they added its compensation, its permanent lining: the maternal receptacle, purified as it might be by the virginal fantasy" (175–176). In Kristeva's interpretation of Christianity in "Stabat Mater," then, woman and religion are structurally, thematically, and logically linked. She reveals a maternal substratum to the paternal Christian discourse, and hints at an association of motherhood, religion, and death.

*Powers of Horror* (1980, trans. 1982) undertakes an inquiry into the maternal mytheme underlying the sense of the sacred and informing the structure of religious ritual. In an inversion of Freud's classic argument in *Totem and Taboo*, Kristeva argues that what religion represses is not a primal parricide but a primal abhorrence of the mother. She examines the confrontation with the maternal, the "coming face to face with the unnameable" (58), the "abject" that she sees at the base of all religions. She discloses this sense of the abject in religious rituals of defilement and purification: "the function of these religious rituals is to ward off the subject's fear of his very own identity sinking irretrievably into the mother . . . risking the loss not of a part (castration) but of the totality of his living being" (64).

Kristeva's abject is a condensation of all fears, a translation, of sorts, of the primal relation to the mother (64). It is, according to Taylor, "what all systems—philosophical, psychological, social, political, economic and religious — are constructed to exclude." (Taylor 1987, 161) Having established the link between the abject and the feminine, Kristeva proceeds to argue: "as abjection—so the sacred. Abjection accompanies all religious constructions" (Taylor 1987, 167).

Through this hermeneutic of abhorrence, the Levitical laws of purity and holiness in the Old Testament are interpreted as fear of the generative and destructive power of the archaic mother. Kristeva finds the Old Testament prophetic call to justice to be based on the same pattern: the fear of the feminine is extended into a theological abhorrence of sin and injustice as impure and necessarily excluded from the holy community (107). Christianity too, as she reads it, is founded on this narcissistic mother-fantasy and its denial, but in the Christian context "the other sex, the feminine, becomes synonymous with a radical evil that is to be suppressed" (70).

In "Women's Time" (1979, trans. 1986), an essay on feminism and modernity, Kristeva evokes the homology of woman and religion in an argument that is somewhat different. Here she describes radical feminism as "religious." In this context its religious dimensions make it dangerous: "The women's movement . . . is situated within the very framework of the religious crisis of our civilization . . . modernity is characterized as the first epoch in human history in which human beings attempt to live without religion. In its present form, is not feminism in the process of becoming one?" (208).

She argues that the first generation of liberal feminists, seeking equality with men, "aspired to gain a place in linear time," while among the second generation of radical feminists, the theorists of *l'écriture féminine*, "linear temporality has been almost totally refused" in an attempt to "give a language to the intrasubjective and corporeal experiences left mute by culture in the past" (194). No proponent of this second-generation feminism, Kristeva warns against its religio-ideological and essentialist "belief in Woman, Her power, Her writing" (208). Describing her deep concern over "second generation feminism" she argues that the logic of reversal used by radical feminists locates them as profound victims of patriarchy. Carried to its anti-sacrificial extremes, the feminist logic of reversal challenges "the very principle of sociality" (208).

She dreams of a third-generation feminism beyond this stance of reversal, a new phase that could "channel this demand for difference into each and every element of the female whole, and finally, bring out the singularity of each woman, and beyond this, her multiplicities, her plural languages, beyond the horizon, beyond sight, beyond faith itself" (208). Paradoxically, at the same time that she imagines this position "beyond faith itself," she also acknowledges the danger that it "might become another form of spiritualism," and she asks, "What discourse, if not that of a religion, would be able to support this adventure?" (210). But whether second-generation feminism is too much like a religion, or third-generation feminism requires the support of the discourse of religion, the structural homology of religion with woman, here transposed into feminism, remains.

Kristeva's lectures on religion, *In the Beginning Was Love: Psychoanalysis and Faith* (1985, trans. 1987) constitute another example of the pattern I am tracing. In this text she seeks the raw material of religious faith and the potential for psychoanalytic cure through the transference relationship in the earliest human experiences of love "close to the maternal container" (26). Without slipping into either a Lacanian denial of pre- or nondiscursive reality or a Winnicottian idealization of this "maternal container," she finds the source of love, ethics, relationship, and faith in a "psychic modality logically and chronologically prior to the sign, to meaning and to the subject." This early psychic stage she describes in terms of Plato's *chora*, "an ancient, mobile, unstable receptacle, prior to the One, to the father, and even to the syllable, metaphorically suggesting something nourishing and maternal" (5).

She returns here to concerns raised in "Stabat Mater." Although the Gospel of John and the Seminars of Jacques (Lacan) would teach "In the Beginning was the Word," Kristeva sees affect, love, and the maternal as always already in language although prior to the word. She reminds us that St. Augustine in *The Confessions* compared Christian faith in God with the infant's relation to its mother's breast. Her interpretation of this text illustrates her understanding of the transformation of nurturant maternal imagery into the paternal structures and symbols of Christianity: "what we have here is fusion with a breast that is, to be sure, succoring, nourishing, loving, protective, but transposed from

the mother's body to an invisible agency located in another world" (24)
—from flesh to word, we might say.

*In the Beginning Was Love* embodies a constant dialectic of "in the
beginning" and "in the end." The end, in this case, is the end of analysis: psychic health. The termination of analysis, made possible by the
verbal and emotional interchanges of the transference relationship, represents the beginning of a new freedom to joyfully engage with the
Other through a kind of reclaiming of illusion not unlike the Winnicottian reaffirmation of illusion. "Analysis must restore to illusion its full
therapeutic and epistemological value," (21) she maintains. But Kristeva's affirmation of illusion goes further than Winnicott's in evoking a
joyous engagement in *jouissance:* "The real end of analysis . . . is that
which comes after a period of disillusionment, when a certain playful-
ness of spirit returns . . . I can also play for real, for keeps, at forming
bonds: creating communities, helping others, loving, losing. Gravity
becomes frivolity that retains its memory of suffering and continues its
search for truth in the joy of perpetually making a new beginning"
(51–52). Kristeva's postanalytic "new beginning" evokes the preanal-
ytic beginning: in the beginning was love, while in the new beginning
are love and language, word and flesh.

Thus these four Kristevan texts, in spite of their divergent arguments and contexts, maintain the homology of woman and religion. In
"Stabat Mater" Kristeva investigates Christianity's discourse surrounding the maternal container enveloping the incarnation of the Word, tracing the religious discourse separating maternal generativity from
death. In *Powers of Horror,* she seeks the source of religious rituals of purity and impurity in the abhorrence of the mother's body as "abject." In
"Women's Time," through a critique of feminism as religion, she warns
against a wish-fulfilling ideology founded on "belief in Woman, Her
power, Her writing." *In the Beginning Was Love* brings a warmer gaze to
both religion and woman, seeking the source of both faith and analytic
transference in a love that is at least metaphorically maternal. Regard-
less of the definition of the terms, their context, or their evaluation, the
pattern I have outlined resists dismantling: the meaning of woman and
the meaning of religion are interlocking pieces of a single structural
unit.

## PART II. THE GENDERING OF ABSENCE

What are we to make of this pattern, evident throughout the texts of
psychoanalysis, associating woman and religion? How can we under-

stand the consistency of this pattern over nearly a century of psychoanalytic formulations? Let me propose that, as Alice Jardine suggests, "the space outside of the conscious subject has always connoted the feminine in the history of Western thought — and any movement into alterity is a movement into that female space" (1986, 565). Woman will always be posited as the ultimate limit to any discourse articulated by man. Woman is the first of such limits — religion is another. All such limits will be gendered as feminine (cf. Jardine 1986, 567).

Van Herik has noted with respect to Freud's texts that "the dilemma presented by Freud, that femininity represents fulfillment in renunciatory culture, might be a useful basis for *asking further questions . . . about how gender works in our moral economy and about how gender and the uses of God are thereby intertwined*" (1982, 200). Van Herik's "further questions" about God and gender represent a form of Freud's question with which we began this inquiry: "What do women want?" Our attention slipped to the form of the question more prominent today, "What does 'woman' mean?" But we found that the question of the meaning of woman always uncovers Van Herik's question: How are God and gender intertwined?

Answers to these questions are always deferred: Freud claims not to know what woman wants, Kristeva and Lacan claim the meaning of woman cannot be spoken, and Van Herik poses but refrains from answering the question about God and gender. I would like to propose that although the answers are *deferred* and the questions *differ,* the answers are just the same: *difference.* Just the same but different: how can the dialogic of sameness and difference illuminate the structural homology I've traced? Having revealed a pattern of identity (woman and religion) in psychoanalytic theory, I want to uncover yet another identity within these two. This identity, in fact, is difference. But difference itself must be examined more closely. As Freud points out, "the danger of incompleteness [in interpretation] is particularly great. One is too easily satisfied with a part explanation, behind which resistance can easily keep back something that may perhaps be more important" (1963, 309). Privileging difference, in my view, becomes a form of resistance that keeps back something (or nothing) more important: namely, absence. Absence is the no-thing upon which the psychoanalytic homology of religion and woman is constructed; difference is that which disguises absence.

In my use of these terms, absence is the otherness or alterity of death or nonbeing, the negation of presence, of life, of being. Difference, on the other hand, is oppositional alterity, hierarchical opposition, or binary separation. The male-female opposition of gender is my primary referent for difference. While some have claimed that the op-position of man and woman is the primordial opposition upon which all others are based, I will argue that presence and absence, formulated as life/death, or being/nonbeing, is, in fact, the primordial opposition. In my view the *difference of gender* serves to disguise *absence in death*. Kris-teva herself notes, "the very dichotomy man-woman as an opposition between two rival entities may be understood as belonging to metaphy-sics" (1986, 209).

How are theories of gender and religion constructed upon differ-ence and absence? Implicit in Freud's texts is the argument that religion provides the discourse that constructs meaning out of absence, non-being, or death. Religion *reconstructs absence as presence:* God exists, you are not alone, you are loved, your suffering is not meaningless, death is not an extinction but a transformation — these religious beliefs, prom-ising presence and negating absence, are the very terms Freud defined as "feminine" illusions in *Future of an Illusion*, insisting upon their "masculine" renunciation in a move that demands the negation of false presence (Van Herik 1982). Paradoxically, what Freud perceived as the solution to the problem of religion he re-created in his analysis of gen-der. He demanded the negation of false (female) presence: he insisted that women admit their "lack" or "absence" in the form of castration, penis envy, maternal absence, wish fulfillment, and irrationality. Thus psychoanalysis theorizes a gendered absence: it creates woman as the privileged paradigm for absence, lack, or death. The psychoanalytic construction of woman as lack makes it possible to speak about differ-ence as female lack without speaking about absence as death; to think about alterity without falling into the gap of death or non-being. Psychoanalysis replaces the religious discourse of absence with a gen-dered discourse of absence.

But this is nothing new. While psychoanalysis theorizes the link between religion and woman, absence and woman, death and woman, the linkage itself is an ancient one. Heretical Gnostic Christians from the early centuries of the common era avoided "the works of woman and the works of death"; orthodox thinkers like the fourth-century Church Father St. John Chrysostom called the female body a "white se-pulcher." Third-century theologian Tertullian stated accusingly to women: "Do you not know that each of you is Eve? . . . You are the dev-il's gateway . . . On account of your desert, that is, death, even the son of God had to die" (Ruether 1974, 197). Similarly, Simone de Beauvoir maintains, "In most popular representations Death is a woman and it is for women to bewail the dead because death is their work. Thus the

Woman-Mother has a face of shadows: she is the chaos whence all have come and whither all must one day return; she is nothingness" (1952, 166).

This ancient tradition of gendering absence, I believe, has performed a two-edged function: the construction of woman as lack may provide a useful defense against death anxiety (especially for men, but perhaps for both men and women), but it also, in my view, contributes to a deeply embedded personal and cultural misogyny. The entanglement of the fear of woman and the fear of death mitigates against the possibility of transcending misogyny. I believe that psychoanalytic theory has begun to bring to the light this ancient and multifaceted connection in a manner that may point toward the possibility of change.

In the pages that follow, I would like to show briefly how Freud, Winnicott, Lacan, and Kristeva construct their linkages of woman and religion upon an underlying notion of absence. The analysis of religion as absence relies primarily on the writings of Freud. Freud shows religion to be the discourse of absence and presence in two ways: first, through the construction of a death-denying afterlife (eternal presence), and second, through its assertion of an eternally present paternal deity. While Freud is the primary psychoanalytic theorist of religion as presence and absence, the linkage of woman with absence draws the attention of all four theorists. Woman is constructed as absence in two ways throughout these theories. First, maternal absence provides the foundation for the construction of the self (Freud and Winnicott) and for the entry into language (Lacan and Kristeva). Second, female castration (absence of the penis) provides the foundation for gender identity (Freud, Lacan, and Kristeva).

I will ask, following Cornell and Thurschwell, "Who is She, the Other of Phallocentric discourse, the mysterious absence that cannot be brought to presence in masculine categories?" (1987, 143). I will argue that, in different ways, each of the four psychoanalytic theorists investigated here reveals that the unnameable Absence of non-being is "named 'woman,' " a move that gives Absence a name, decreasing our terror of it, but simultaneously associates woman with the unnameable, increasing our terror of her.

Woman as absence, man as presence, "feminine" religion as the denial of absence, "masculine" reason as the renunciation of false presence . . . Freud's texts are full of these linkages. Freud's "discovery" of the death instinct, *thanatos,* in *Beyond the Pleasure Principle,* is occasioned by his observation of his grandson's experience of maternal absence. In the repetitious game of "fort" and "da," the child throws and retrieves a spool, recapitulating the absence and longed-for return of the mother. The mother's absence is the stimulus for the repetition compulsion, the desire to have control over what one cannot control, over absence and loss, and thus the stimulus for *thanatos* itself (*Beyond the Pleasure Principle* 18:14–15).

The cornerstone of Freudian theory, the castration complex, also expresses this gendering of absence and presence. Maleness is presence, femaleness is absence. The penis embodies presence: it is there ("da"), it is visible; its absence ("fort") in the girl indicates not the presence of different genitals, but the absence of male genitals. Freud speaks of the "momentous discovery which little girls are destined to make. They notice the penis of a brother or playmate, strikingly visible and of large proportions, (and) at once recognize it as the superior counterpart of their own small and inconspicuous organ" ("Some Psychical Consequences of the Anatomical Distinction between the Sexes" 19:252). Female genitals in Freud's analysis, and even more so in Lacan's, are a gap, a lack, an absence: the female "acknowledges the fact of her castration, and with it, too, the superiority of the male and her own inferiority" ("Female Sexuality" 21:229). In the psychic economy of the male, the female is castrated and castrating, an embodiment of absence, frightening to men because she arouses castration anxiety.

One of Freud's most lyrical analyses of the association of woman with absence/death is in the essay "The Theme of the Three Caskets." He describes the motif, widespread in folktale, literature, and myth, in which the hero must choose the correct casket in order to win the bride. Freud traces a double reversal of destiny in the narrative. First, the myth reverses reality, giving the hero a choice: "choice stands in the place of necessity, of destiny." Second, the myth transforms destiny's gift from death into love: "thus man overcomes death . . . no greater triumph of wish fulfillment is conceivable" (1963:76). The three caskets he sees as the three forms of the mother: "it is the three forms taken on by the figure of the mother as life proceeds: the mother herself, the beloved who is chosen after her pattern, and finally the Mother Earth who receives him again. But it is in vain that the old man yearns after the love of woman as he once had it from his mother; the third of the Fates alone, the silent goddess of Death, will take him into her arms" (76). From the mother or the beloved bride to the silent goddess of death, from *eros* to *thanatos*: the homology could hardly be more explicit.

Freud theorizes absence and presence in other contexts as well as gender—notably, in the arena of consciousness/unconsciousness, and reason/religion. But gender is always just below the surface of these structures; maleness and femaleness are immanent in every construction of presence and absence. The presence Freud embraces is a fragile presence, a presence perched at the boundary of absence: maleness is constantly threatened by femaleness/castration/impotence; (masculine) consciousness is always at the mercy of (feminine) unconsciousness; (masculine) rationality is always endangered by (feminine) wishes; life as presence is always threatened by death/absence (see Laplanche, Van Herik, and Rieff).

The paradox of renunciation demands comment. The renunciation of wishes is the willing abandonment of false presence, the willing embrace of absence. Just as the child throws the spool recapitulating maternal absence in the game of "fort-da"; just as the hero willingly chooses the casket of love/death that destiny will eventually provide; just as the autonomous individual in the utopian world of *Future of an Illusion* abandons the illusion of eternal life; similarly, the mature male renounces willingly the false presence (beliefs, illusions, attachments) that he will inevitably lose. Renunciation represents a kind of absence in presence, an acceptance or affirmation of absence. It is a choice of death in the face of the inevitable, a "carrying back of death into life" (Laplanche 1976, 123).

Religion for Freud is false presence. It denies the absence of death with the promise of *eternal presence* (as eternal life); it denies *maternal absence* with the promise of (divine) *paternal presence*. Freud's normative ideal of renunciatory reason is an embrace of limited presence. Reason, according to Freud, must be always ready to renounce its own claims, acknowledging that what we deeply desire is presence, and that what we are constantly fending off is absence. Freud thus theorizes presence and absence in such texts as *Future of an Illusion, Beyond the Pleasure Principle*, and *Female Sexuality*, subtly gendering both: the female is absent (castrated), the mother is absent ("fort"); religion is the (feminine) false promise of presence, the empty promise of a victory of presence (eternal life) over absence (death, non-being).

Winnicott is also a theorist of presence and absence, although his tendency is to subsume absence in presence. If the mother of the newborn is the ever-present mother, the good-enough mother is often absent, and it is her very absence that makes possible the "transitional objects," symbolizing the mother-in-absence and leading to a separate sense of self and to culture itself. The child, the self, can truly be born only when the mother has withdrawn — there is no *being*, no sense of self, without maternal absence. But this separation is not usually catastrophic. Maternal absence is benign, necessary, even creative, unless pushed to the extremes of abandonment or neglect. Rather than the Freudian spool that is thrown "fort" and pulled "da" as a metaphor of control over maternal absence, Winnicott's favored metaphor for control over maternal absence is the teddy bear—always "da," never "fort," a "good enough" replacement for the mother. God, religion, and culture are, like the teddy bear, substitutes for maternal absence, illusory transitional objects (see Rizzuto 1979).

In Winnicott's revision of psychoanalytic theory, then, just as in Freud's *Beyond the Pleasure Principle*, the woman-religion homology is constructed upon a conceptualization of maternal absence. And again like Freud, Winnicott extends his analysis of maternal absence to a homology with death: "when the mother is away . . . she is dead from the point of view of the child. This is what dead means. It is a matter of days or hours or minutes. Before the limit is reached the mother is still alive; after this limit has been overstepped she is dead" (1971, 21–22).

If Freud and Winnicott construct their homologies of woman and religion upon a foundation of maternal or feminine absence, Lacan similarly grounds his discussions of woman and religion in absence. He extends his analysis of absence to its extreme form in death less often than Freud, although as we have seen he links woman, misogyny ("dit-femme, difamme"), and the denial of death in his discussion of the immortality of the soul (1982, 156). But Lacan is a theorist of absence par excellence. He engages directly the question of absence as otherness and alterity, theorizing the gendering of alterity, of the unconscious, and of god.

For Lacan, according to Winquist, "what is discovered (through psychoanalysis) is not what is present. What is discovered is an absence" (1989, 29). For Lacan, "the reality of the unconscious . . . is not an ambiguity of acts, future knowledge that is already known not to be known, but lacunae, with rupture inscribed in a certain lack" (Lacan 1981, 25). In Lacan's theory, as in Winnicott's, maternal absence is the condition of be-ing: the birth of the subject and entry into the realm of language involves a traumatic separation from the maternal matrix, a loss of the archaic mother. "The child can be born only when the mother withdraws her breast. Everything begins with a catastrophic cleavage" (Taylor 1987, 88). The Lacanian maternal absence is more traumatic than Winnicott's benign maternal absence. Language, or the word of the father, severs the mother-child binary. By barring a return to the mother, the father makes irrecoverable the infant's loss of maternal presence. The child loses "the experience of wholeness, the sense of being one with the mother. The pain of this loss results in a primary repression that on one hand buries the memory of the relationship to the archaic mother in the unconscious, and on the other hand catapults the infant into the symbolic realm of meaningful discourse in order to fulfill its desire to reestablish a relation with an other . . . this desire can never be satisfied" (Cornell and Thurschwell 1987, 145).

Lacan constructs a multilayered negation of maternal presence through the notion of the "phallic mother," the phantasmatic image of wholeness through the symbiotic relation with the mother. Maternal presence is negated through the inevitable and cataclysmic loss of relationship described above. It is also negated through the de-gendering of the archaic mother: Lacan makes the archaic mother a "phallic mother." Although he insists that the phallus is not the penis (1977, 285), nevertheless, the slippage from phallus to penis is frequent in Lacan's texts (Gallop 1985, 133–156). Maternality thus embodies absence through association with the penis/phallus that erases her gender. In addition, maternality embodies absence through association with the illusory presence of the Lacanian "Phallus," since the Phallus as privileged signifier (1977, 287) signifies the *false* sense of unity, fullness, reality, or presence in signification. Finally, the phallic mother embodies absence through an association with castration as well: "with the notion of the 'phallic mother' Lacan extends the Freudian notion of castration from the difference of genders to the genesis of the symbolic realm of language. In place of the infant's discovery of the lack of a phallus, he substitutes the infant's discovery of the lack of the 'phallic mother' " (Cornell and Thurschwell 1987, 146). Although his analysis of castration deflects attention from the penis and redirects it to the linguistic, symbolic "phallus" of language, meaning, and signification, he consistently defines the mother or the woman in terms of absence.

If the phallic mother is veiled, castrated, and castrating (Lacan 1977, 322), and "woman" in Lacan's analysis does not exist, woman nevertheless "figures" or "represents" radical otherness or Alterity. The Lacanian homology of God and Woman discussed above rests upon an understanding of Lacanian Otherness and unconscious. For Lacan, the unconscious is the "desire of the Other," "the language of the other." The unconscious is radically other; it is God, and it is also, for Lacan, eternally feminine. Centering on otherness, alterity, absence, and lack, Lacan makes "woman" the privileged metaphor for this alterity.

If Lacan is the theorist who grounds woman and God most clearly in alterity, Kristeva locates the homology most explicitly in death. We have seen her investigation in "Stabat Mater" of Christianity's inversion of the woman/death homology in the cult of the Virgin Mary. In Black Sun, she notes, "Freudian theory detects everywhere the same impos-

sible mourning for the maternal object" (1989, 13). She returns to
Freud's insistence that, though death may be unrepresentable, it is displaced metonymically onto a number of symbolic representations.
"Freud found in imaginary productions, religions, art, literature . . . a
kind of representation of death anxiety" (1989, 26). The most important
displacement or representation of death, however, is in "woman": "the
unrepresentable nature of death was linked with that other unrepresentable — original abode but also last resting place for dead souls, in
the beyond — which for mythical thought is constituted by the female
body" (27). Castration fear is one of the forms this female-directed
death anxiety can take. "The horror of castration underlying the anguish of death undoubtedly accounts in large part for the *universal partnership with death of the penis-lacking feminine*" (27: emphasis added). She
adds another element to this partnership, however, insisting that the
image of the death-bearing woman, the feminine as the image of death,
is the screen not only for the fear of castration, but, more important, it
is also a screen for matricide: "For man and for woman the loss of the
mother is a biological and psychic necessity, the first step on the way to
becoming autonomous. Matricide is our vital necessity, the *sine qua non*
of our individuation. . . . The feminine as image of death is . . . an imaginary safety catch for the matricidal drive that, without such a representation, would pulverize me into melancholia if it did not drive me to
crime" (27–28).

Kristeva sees the image of death as feminine as a positive, beneficial, even miraculous, image: "the imaginary capability of western
man, which is fulfilled within Christianity, is the ability to transfer
meaning to the very place where it was lost in death and/or nonmean-
ing . . . (it) constitutes a miracle" (103). In her view, the image of death
as feminine provides a protection against collapse into meaningless-
ness: "By representing that unsymbolized as a maternal object, a
source of sorrow and nostalgia, but of ritual veneration as well, the melancholy imagination sublimates it and gives itself a protection against
collapsing into a-symbolism" (165). Similarly, she argues for the necessity of the "phallic mother" as a defense against nothingness: "If the
mother were not, that is, if she were not phallic, then every speaker
would be led to conceive of its Being in relation to some Void, a nothingness asymmetrically opposed to this Being, a permanent threat against
first its mastery, and ultimately, its stability" ("Motherhood According
to Giovanni Bellini" 1980, 238).

Kristeva accurately reveals the power and ubiquity of the image of
death as female. What our other three psychoanalysts expressed im-
plicitly she makes explicit. But Kristeva's belief in the beneficial qualities

and the inevitability of this image of woman as death are deeply problematic. The symbolic and eroticized image of woman as death may keep the melancholic away from suicidal self-destruction (1989, 28), but in my view this image lies at the heart of two central cultural problems: it is at the core of our deep-rooted misogyny, and it obstructs our ability to embrace death as absence, extinction, or nonbeing.

Freud's observation of a certain repetition associated with the mother led to his construction of the death instinct, *thanatos.* Our observation of a certain repetition associated with the mother (and religion) also led to the discovery of death. Death, the unrepresentable, the ultimate absence, is symbolized as woman; woman becomes, through metonymy, death. Maternal absence, matricide, and castration (absence as female), are negated in the religious promise of presence through eternal life and paternal love (presence as male). The psychoanalytic theories examined here have disclosed a complex weaving of life and death, male and female, presence and absence, in a process that leads to the internalization of the image of woman as death.

This disturbing image points toward another answer to the questions we posed earlier: Freud's question, what do women want; the contemporary question, what does woman mean, and Van Herik's question, how are god and gender intertwined. The *difference* indicated above as a tentative answer to these questions does indeed approach the heart of the issue: the difference of absolute absence in death is conflated with the differences of opposition in gender. Through our readings of these psychoanalytic theories, these questions can now be answered: according to (male fears in) phallocentric culture, what "women" want is death; what "woman" means is death, and god and gender are interwined in death.

This psychoanalytic construction of woman as death functions both to continue the tradition expressing misogyny and death anxiety by constructing woman as absence, *and* to subvert or expose misogyny and death anxiety by showing how woman and absence have been homologized, making possible a critique of the homology. Psychoanalysis did not invent or create the connection between woman and death; rather, it disclosed a persistent pattern. Kristeva sees this as a universal pattern—a "universal partnership." However, I see this partnership as a sociohistorically limited one. This partnership of woman and death articulates the gendering of absence in phallocentric culture—but it is by no means universal (see DuBois 1988, 187).

The insight of psychoanalytic theory lies in its description of the way that the *religious and metaphysical language of presence and absence in western culture is/has become the language of gender.* If the discourse of gender as absence once *supplemented* the religious discourse of absence, I believe that the discourse of gender as absence now moves toward *replacing* the religious discourse of absence. A close reading of the psychoanalytic texts on gender, religion, and absence may ultimately reveal a path beyond the fear of woman and the fear of death through the disentanglement of gender and religion.

The gendering of absence, or more specifically the feminizing of absence as lack, is what links religion to women in the four psychoanalytic theories I've traced. Gender supplements religion in generating a secondary discourse of presence and absence that comes to be seen as the primary discourse of presence and absence. Gayle Rubin has argued that "gender is a socially imposed division of the sexes ... Men and women are of course, different. But they are not as different as day and night, earth and sky, yin and yang, life and death. In fact ... men and women are closer to each other than either is to anything else" (1975, 179). Yet the sameness of men and women is denied in a discourse of difference focusing on woman as absence, a discourse that conflates woman with death and man with life.

Although psychoanalytic theorists typically have not seen their primary task as an inquiry into the sources of sexism in western culture, nevertheless, current psychoanalytic investigations have moved toward addressing the problem of misogyny, offering provocative analyses of the structures and workings of culture and psyche. Some have argued that psychoanalysis generates and promotes misogyny, but others, like Mitchell (1974, 1982) Rose (1982), Van Herik (1982), and Kofman (1985) have shown that psychoanalysis reveals the intricate workings of cultural, social, and psychic structures — structures that can be changed if they are understood. In my view, psychoanalysis has accurately described a metonymic association of woman and religion, which, through a careful reading, can be shown to rest upon a linkage of both woman and religion with absence/death. Rather than following Kristeva's lead and toward a celebration of his metonymy by seeking a beneficial "safety catch" in it, let us instead pursue the "via negativa" mapped out by Kristeva in another cartography. "We may say," she suggested, subtly echoing the Vedantic Neti, Neti, " 'That's not it!' and 'That's still not it!' " (Marks 1981, 137). Let us then, inquire into the question of the relation of this metonymy to misogyny and to absence, considering how absence in death might be symbolized without recourse to the differences of gender and how the differences of gender might be dissociated from absence in death.

*The author would like to thank Professor Marilyn Edelstein of Santa Clara University for reading and responding to many drafts of the paper.

## ( INTER-TEXT 1 )

The premise of this essay rests on Judith Van Herik's *Freud on Femininity and Faith*, with its argument that Freud systematically associates religious (especially Christian) belief, in its wishful, illusory character, with the traits he also characteristically assigns to the feminine. Jonte-Pace finds this correlation repeated, with different valuations and functions, in Winnicott and again in Lacan. Kristeva's consideration of Mary in "Stabat Mater," her analysis in *Powers of Horror* of maternal abjection as the root of the distinction between the holy (sacred) and the impure, her discernment of a religious dimension to some feminisms in "Women's Time," and the maternal dimension of transference, for both psychoanalysis and faith, in *In the Beginning was Love*, all in quite different ways continue this religious-feminine association.

The root of this persistent homology, she holds, is the status of the feminine as the different. In patriarchal culture, in language as the law of the father, the feminine is the sphere of what is not representable, calculable, symbolically controllable—it becomes the primordial metaphor of difference. Difference, in turn, is a screen for absence, for death: "Difference of gender serves to disguise absence in death." Religion, through its construction of death as transformation, "reconstructs absence as presence" and thus is functionally equivalent to the feminine metaphor. "Psychoanalysis replaces the religious discourse of absence with a gendered discourse of absence."

The dialectic of wishful illusion (false presence) and renunciation (consent to absence) is articulated with Freud's account of the "fort-da" game of the child with the spool in *Beyond the Pleasure Principle*. Religion is for Freud false presence, the denial of maternal absence. Absence, castration, death are the determining qualities of woman for this constellation. In Winnicott, rather than the dialectic of presence and absence, we have the transitional object as substitute presence—God, in this model, is the transitional object par excellence. And for Lacan language separates mother and child, and is thus haunted by maternal absence as its other, as the figure for everything language is not.

In *Black Sun*, Kristeva explicitly examines this homology and finds in the feminine as image of death a "safety catch for the matricidal

drive" whose roots she had analyzed especially in *Powers of Horror.*
Jonte-Pace finds in this positive valuation of the woman-death homology two key problems: its support for our cultural mysogyny and its ob-
scuring of the truth of death as extinction. It is her hope that this com-
bination can be disentangled to open a path beyond fear of woman and
fear of death.

In the course of her discussion, Jonte-Pace refers to Mark Taylor's
discussions of Lacan and Kristeva in *Altarity.* Taylor, there and in his
contribution to *Lacan and Theological Discourse,* appears to make a homology of woman and difference such as Jonte-Pace criticizes. An interesting conversation should be possible between Jonte-Pace and Taylor
around this topic. Extending such a conversation to the consideration of
the ambiguant relation of woman and difference developed here, and
Jonte-Pace's exposure of the duplicitous supplementarity of woman/
other/sacred in our discourse, might also give us further insight into the
theological import of the work of Taylor's mentor Derrida.

The question of illusion figures in several of our essays. But only
here is the concept of illusion itself examined and thematized in its role
as figuring the presence of the absent mother and the denial of death.
Ernest Becker's thesis, that religion is illusion necessitated by the fact
that the truth of our death (and animality) is unbearable, is in the same
territory with Jonte-Pace's discussion. (And despite his Freudian prem-
ises, Becker does not adopt the feminizing model but rather affirms the
conception of a heroic illusion that accepts its own fictive character and
embraces as much as possible of life and society, in a style more mono-
lithic than Kristeva's but following the same direction. Cleo Kearns
touches on this question, and I return to Becker in commenting on her
essay.)

Jonte-Pace has discussed Kristeva's analysis of abjection in *Powers
of Horror,* but it might be argued that she has not given it sufficient
weight. Martha Reineke's essay examines the question in more detail,
and David Fisher also makes use of it. If abjection is rooted in the semiotic significance of bodily separation from mother, in birth, weaning,
conflict, absence, then misogyny and a maternal/abject covering over
the issue of death would seem to be inescapable. Jonte-Pace is right that
these are central cultural problems. But Kristeva's analysis suggests
that they can not be supplanted but, at best, sublimated—through imagery such as the Mary of "Stabat Mater" or "Motherhood According
to Giovanni Bellini," or the maternal Father of Johannine theology, or
more artistic and plural alternatives. One must not, perhaps, settle easily for that, but establishing the space for an alternative that did not con-

join woman and death might be aided by a further substantial and rigorous analysis of the archaic territory Kristeva addresses.

If there is a way beyond here, it might lie in consideration of what Kristeva in *Tales of Love* calls "the zero degree of subjectivity." At the originary site of the subject, there is a gap, a void, that comes to be covered over by an imaginary identification with mother's other. If nothingness is not to be modeled on mother's absence, it comes back home to the central nothingness of subjectivity itself. In a sense, it is the necessity to represent nothingness as *something else* in order to maintain the cover over the central void that founds the abjection of mother. Jonte-Pace's desire to get beyond that abjection is thus aimed at the core of our resistance, our own nothingness. This core, and its cover, precede our own knowledge of death and line its significance for us, so perhaps the homology of inner nothingness and maternal abjection is even more primordial than the question of death.

# METAPHOR, META-NARRATIVE, AND MATER-NARRATIVE IN KRISTEVA'S "STABAT MATER"[1]

## Marilyn Edelstein

*While Jonte-Pace has begun with a wide circle through psychoanalytic theories prior to Kristeva and then zeroed in on a core problematic, Marilyn Edelstein proceeds by a different route. She begins with a single Kristevan text, "Stabat Mater," which Jonte-Pace has also discussed. She situates that text in a literary rather than psychoanalytic community of discussion. Where Jonte-Pace began with the question of woman and pursued it to the heart of the problem of the mother, Edelstein begins with the figure of the mother and examines, among other themes, its suitability as an image for woman. The question of mother as metaphor raises the general question of metaphor. The problem of the split subject is examined in the textual split effected in this intermittently two-column text. The problem of language as mastery, which in Jonte-Pace is a theme taken from Lacan as background for the Kristevan discussion, here becomes a question of Kristeva's writing and a question of our reading.*

Borders, thresholds, folds, crossroads, crosses — all have been recurrent metaphors of intersection and confluence (themselves metaphors) in Julia Kristeva's writings.[2] Her work on language, borderline patients, literary limit-texts, the maternal, the abject, and faith is united by an interest in what exists at and beyond the boundaries of human experience. Much of her work has explored those processes through which (subject/object) boundaries are both broached and maintained dialogically and relationally.

Her own border crossings brought her from Bulgaria to Paris in 1965[3]; her vast body of work transgresses (from the Latin, *trānsgredī*, to step across) boundaries, too, fluidly moving between structuralism and poststructuralism, modernism and postmodernism, philosophy and literature, religion and psychoanalysis.

Kristeva's work itself seems to have reached a crossroads in the mid- to late 1970s. The '70s were a productive period for her, as she became both a practicing psychoanalyst and a mother, and wrote several important books and numerous articles. Some see this period as one of subtle reconfiguration of her interests. Others, more critical, see the '70s as marking the break between the prelapsarian (materialist, political) Kristeva and the lapsarian (individualist, antipolitical) Kristeva. Paul Smith, for instance, condemns "the deplorable turn of Kristeva's work of late" ("Julia Kristeva Et Al." 98).[4]

Her border crossings have made Kristeva's work a major site of intellectual contestation, especially among feminists and Marxists.[5] Is Kristeva a post-Marxist or an anti-Marxist? A feminist, post-feminist, or anti-feminist? Why has a theorist once so interested in linguistic and political transgressions of the "sociosymbolic contract" turned her attention increasingly to theorizing about maternity, love, and faith?

Such critics as Smith and Ann Rosalind Jones see her increasing interest in motherhood, individual psyches, and religion as both interrelated and troublingly conservative.[6] Even more sympathetic commentators find it difficult to deal with the shifts in Kristeva's concerns. Has the former *materialist* become a *maternalist?* Although only one letter separates these two terms, both from the same root, *mater,* they imply radical differences in perspective.

Certainly, there are both continuities and ruptures in her work from the 1960s to the 1990s. Her interests, though, have always focused on "the system and the speaking subject" (the title of a 1973 essay); perhaps the emphasis has simply changed from the former to the latter. Her style, too, has changed, becoming less rigorously and abstractly philosophical (perhaps Hegelian) and more lyrical, poetic, associative (perhaps more Sollerian).[7]

Her innovative essay, "Stabat Mater," written in 1977, seems to be a locus for the various crossings in her work I've noted, and especially for her interests in the (intersecting) discourses of motherhood, love, the avant-garde, and religion. In this essay on the Virgin Mother and on (m)otherhood, numerous Kristevan themes and styles — from all phases of her career—intersect. Just as Kristeva has been focusing more and more on the individual, the singular, the specific, I'd like to examine this specific essay as a way of exploring Kristeva's transgressions more generally.

In "Stabat Mater," Julia Kristeva simultaneously theorizes, narrates, and enacts the discourses of the (m)other. Unlike most psychoanalytic theorists, who focus on the mother as *object* for the child, Kristeva here emphasizes the mother as *subject,* the mother's own experience of her maternity and of her relation to her child and her own body (and to her own mother). Kristeva attempts to create more a discourse of *maternality-for-the-mother* than of *maternality-for-the-other.* But in order to do so, she must also examine what she sees as perhaps the most powerful Western symbol of maternality-for-the-other, the Virgin Mary.

As Kristeva notes, "there is no secular discourse on the psychology of motherhood," but Christianity, and particularly Catholicism, has provided an elaborate discourse on Motherhood, as exemplified by the Virgin Mary (*In the Beginning* 43). In "Stabat Mater," though, religious discourse *about* the mother must coexist with a parallel discourse (in a separate column) *by* a mother. This essay's narrative strategies and construction of both its speaking and reading subject(s) are as much part of its meaning as —and inseparable from—its propositional statements or theses, and I'd like to analyze both here.

The maternal has become a central concern of Kristeva's latest work and of criticism of it. The mother and the maternal are themselves sites of intersection, of boundary crossing, of transgression, in her analyses. I'd like to explore here the intimate relations in Kristeva's work, especially in "Stabat Mater," between the maternal and love, ethics, metaphor, faith, and the avant-garde—all dialogically constituted sites (or processes) of encounter between subject and other. In Kristeva's work, the maternal may serve as a metaphor for metaphor and perhaps even for the split subject itself. If this is so, the maternal metaphor need not be seen as essentialist or as glorifying or even linked to the biological act of childbearing.[8] But can a biological metaphor ever be completely severed from biology? Where *does* "the mother" stand in "Stabat Mater"?

Kristeva's essay is named for the Latin hymn to Mary's suffering at the Crucifixion; it was titled "Hérethique de l'amour" when it first appeared in *Tel Quel* in 1977, then renamed upon its inclusion in *Histoires d'amour.*[9] It begins as a theoretical and historical essay on "the maternal," as symbolized in the Christian construct of the Virgin Mary, and on the psychic and social needs its transmutations have reflected and served in western culture. Although the essay begins with conventional typography, in a "FLASH" a new second column is soon born on the left, in bold typeface, that seems to recount lyrically and impressionistically the speaker's own bodily and psychic experiences surrounding and including the birth of her son. This personal reflection on and narrative of motherhood weaves in and out of the analytical text, which sometimes becomes the sole text when the left-hand text disappears or, occasionally, mimics the right-hand "voice." Perhaps the essay is, like Pergolesi's hymn *Stabat Mater,* a duet as well as a juxtaposition of two solo voices.[10]

This generically and stylistically experimental essay is Kristeva's first to leave the densely theoretical style of particularly her early semiological writing for a more avant-garde, postmodern style.[11] Kristeva has called postmodernist texts "writing-as-experience-of-limits," "that literature which writes itself with the more or less conscious intention of expanding the signifiable and thus human realm" ("Postmodernism?" 137). She also interprets such texts' style "as an exploration of the typical imaginary relationship, that to the mother, through the most radical and problematic aspect of this relationship, language" (139–140). Kristeva has linked the avant-garde and "the women's struggle" ("Woman can never be defined" 139), since they can both be practices of "rupture and negativity" ("Oscillation" 167). It's interesting, given these linkages between "woman" and literary/linguistic limits, that Kristeva's first postmodern theoretical essay itself concerns motherhood.

If it's postmodern, though, is it also feminist or even "feminine"? The essay's flouting of generic convention is typical of both postmodern and some feminist discourse. At first, the essay's "personal/theoretical" typographical dualism might seem an obvious, even clichéd, ploy. I think this essay can be seen as both exemplifying and parodying *écriture féminine* (which she sees as indebted to male experimentalists like Mallarmé and Joyce anyway). Parody generally signals ambivalence — both distance from and attachment to the parodied text. In essays like "Women's Time," Kristeva has criticized attempts at such "feminine writing," which relies on a "belief in Woman, Her power, Her writing" with which it needs to "break free" (208); yet she acknowledges that sexual difference "translates [into] . . . a difference, then, in the relationship to power, language and meaning" (196).

"Stabat Mater's" left column does seem more like a text by Cixous or Irigaray than a typical Kristeva essay — but this column does not stand alone. Thus Kristeva can avoid what she criticizes in other French feminists — the "Manichean position which consists in designating as feminine" *only* those aspects of language having to do with "the imprecise, . . . with impulses, perhaps with primary processes." This linkage of the feminine and the "unsayable" winds up "maintaining women in a position of inferiority, and, in any case, of marginality" ("Two Interviews" 122–23). Instead, Kristeva puts the two columns in a dialogic relationship, as I'll elaborate below.

The essay transgresses boundaries between theory and literature, as well as between the personal and the abstract, the subjective and the social, the semiotic and the symbolic. The text is concretely transgressive, as words, images, ideas cross over from one column to the other. It may be transgressive, too, in Kristeva's positive sense of confounding the limits of the symbolic through the incursions of the semiotic.

For Kristeva, like Lacan, the "symbolic" is the realm of language and culture, the law of the Father. Her "semiotic"—which has no precise parallel in Lacan's three-part scheme of Imaginary, Symbolic, and Real—is the realm of the body, the drives, the unconscious.[12] For Kristeva, the semiotic "logically and chronologically precedes the establishment of the symbolic and its subject . . . " (*Revolution in Poetic Language* 41), yet the symbolic and the semiotic permanently and dynamically coexist, in the subject and in language. As Kristeva puts it, "these two modalities are inseparable within the *signifying process* that constitutes language" (*Revolution* 24). In its sensuousness, rhythm, musicality, language is semiotic; the symbolic is the level of meaning in language. Although Kristeva refers to the relation between the semiotic and symbolic in language as a "dialectic" (24), the relationship actually seems more dialogic. The very structure of "Stabat Mater" embodies (entexts?) this dialogue between the semiotic and the symbolic.

The concept of the dialogic or dialogism derives from the work of Mikhail Bakhtin (particularly in *The Dialogic Imagination*). Kristeva first introduced Bakhtin's work to a western audience when she wrote about his dialogic theory of the novel in her *Séméiotiké* in 1969. As Paul de Man notes, Bakhtin's notion of the "dialogic" moved (in Bakhtin's own work and in other theorists' uses of the term) from describing a primarily "intralinguistic" (and specifically novelistic) relationship "between what he calls two heterogeneous 'voices,' " to evoking far more broadly the "principle of radical otherness or, to use again Bakhtin's own terminology, as a principle of *exotopy*" (108–09), or "outsideness." Many of Kristeva's concepts, too, like negativity or the subject itself, migrate from a linguistic or literary context to a broader psychoanalytic or philosophical or cultural one. For Bakhtin, like Kristeva, the "intralinguistic" cannot be separated from, and is homologous to, the "extralinguistic," since language is the very foundation of sociality.[13] Linguistic and literary practice both reflect and shape social practice.

In "Word, Dialogue, and Novel," Kristeva identifies Bakhtinian dialogism with both intersubjectivity and intertextuality (a term she's usually credited with inventing, but for which she credits Bakhtin). She notes that Bakhtin believes dialogism is "inherent in language itself" (68). In literary discourse (and, by extrapolation, in all discourse), dialogism signals "another logic ... the logic of *distance and relationship* ... in opposition to the level of continuity and substance, both of which obey the logic of being and are thus monological." This "other logic" is one "of *analogy and nonexclusive opposition*, opposed to monological levels of causality and identifying determination" (71–72). She also writes of "the psychic aspect of writing as trace of a dialogue with oneself (with another), as a writer's distance from himself, as a splitting of the writer into subject of enunciation and subject of utterance" (74). Certainly, these elements of dialogism — as dynamic, relational, nonidentitarian, heterogeneous — link the concept to more familiar Kristevan notions of negativity, splitting, transgression, process.

I'd like to suggest that much of Kristeva's later work, spiraling out from linguistics, has been profoundly influenced by her early work on Bakhtin; as she says, Bakhtin introduced her to "the notion of *alterity* and *dialogism*" ("My Memory's Hyperbole" 267). The relationships between the subject (especially the mother) and the other (and between the subject and itself), between reading and writing, between the semiotic and symbolic are all dialogic, in Kristevan theory.[14]

*Dialogism* here is not to be confused with *binarism* nor with Hegelian (or Marxist) *dialectic*. As Katerina Clark and Michael Holquist note, Bakhtin "emphasizes performance, history, actuality, and the openness of dialogue, as opposed to the closed dialectic of Structuralism's binary oppositions." Bakhtin, they argue, "makes the enormous leap from dialectical, or partitive thinking, which is still presumed to be the universal norm, to dialogic or relational thinking" (7).

Kristeva, too, differentiates the dialogic, which respects difference, from Hegelian dialectic, which she sees as "based on a triad and thus on struggle and projection, a movement of transcendence," and still firmly within Aristotelian logic. Dialogism, on the other hand, "replaces these concepts by absorbing them within the concept of *relation*. It does not strive towards transcendence but rather toward harmony, all the while implying an idea of rupture ... as a modality of transformation" ("Word" 88–9, my emphasis).[15] Relation and rupture are certainly common Kristevan themes; perhaps the stranger notion of harmony becomes subsumed, finally, in her concept of love, which the mother incarnates.

Which brings us back to "Stabat Mater," in which Kristeva theorizes about mothers, others, and the love and space between and within them. She begins, appropriately, with a question: "If it is not possible to say of a *woman* what she *is* (without running the risk of abolishing her difference), would it perhaps be different concerning the *mother,* since that is the only function of the 'other sex' to which we can definitely attribute existence?" (161). Kristeva will attempt to say what the figure of the woman Mary, paradoxically both virgin and mother, has signified within Western discourse.[16] Mary has also been presented, paradoxically, both as unique, "alone among women" and also as an idealized model for all women, or at least all mothers — loving, understanding, and supremely self-sacrificing — a mother purely for others.

In the right-hand column of "Stabat Mater," Kristeva analyzes three major themes in the "incredible construct of the Maternal that the West elaborated by means of the Virgin" (179), "one of the most powerful imaginary constructs known in the history of civilizations" (163). First, Kristeva discusses the Church's views of Mary's immaculate conception (which only formally became dogma in 1854). Asserting Mary's immaculate conception, by making her sexless, would link her to Jesus and sinlessness and, finally, deathlessness, through Assumption, which only was proclaimed dogma in 1950; Kristeva asks, "What death anguish was it intended to soothe after the conclusion of the deadliest of wars?" (169). Secondly, in a much briefer section, Kristeva discusses the image of Mary's power as queen (both earthly and divine), and the ways in which this view could strengthen the church's own earthly powers. Lastly, Kristeva discusses Mary as the "prototype of love," particularly seen as sacrifice.[17]

Kristeva's discussion of love in the Marian myth and in women's, and especially mothers', lives, constitutes the largest section of the essay — in both columns; love is a central issue in much of her recent writing. Yet, she doesn't idealize love (or the maternal).[18] In her analysis, maternal love is a form of sacrifice and produces an acute sense of both identification and separation, of narcissism and masochism, of pleasure and pain.

Maternal *jouissance,* the intense sensual pleasure of mothering, is announced in the left columns ("he dances in my neck, flutters with my hair ... sweetness of the child ... " [171]), but so is the assertion that "a mother is always branded by pain" (167), as Mary was by her son's death even as He became immortal. Making the homology with Mary *and* with her son even more explicit, Kristeva writes that mothers "live on that border, crossroads beings, crucified beings" (178).[19] Although Kristeva locates such "crucifixion" in mothering, her texts suggest that all (split) subjects exist at such crossroads between pain and pleasure, lack and plenitude, sameness and difference.[20]

Although Kristeva believes the Virgin Mary construct in some ways served "women's wishes for identification," it primarily functioned to stabilize society, for instance, through mediating between the "unconscious needs of primary narcissism" and a society requiring "the contribution of the superego and . . . the symbolic paternal agency" (182). Kristeva is interested also in those symbolic needs the Virgin Mary myth hasn't met, or has ceased to meet for most twentieth-century women. Prominent by its absence is any discourse of the Other Woman — of women's relationship both to their own mothers and to Woman as an abstraction and a collectivity. She critiques and tries to fill this gap, much as she does the gap in Freud where a theory of motherhood itself might (should?) have been: "The fact remains, as far as the complexities and pitfalls of maternal experience are involved, that Freud offers only a massive *nothing* . . . " ("Stabat" 178–79).[21]

Her discussion of the relation to "the other" leads into her final, suggestive remarks on the concerns of the essay's original title — with love and "heretical ethics" or "herethics," a new ethical conception based on woman as mother, as a prototype or metaphor for one who deals with the other through love. Kristeva writes that "maternity is a bridge between singularity and ethics" ("A New Type of Intellectual" 297). For Kristeva, the ethical consists in "reaching out to the other" ("Stabat" 182).

At the end of "Stabat Mater," when she proposes "a contemporary ethics," "an heretical ethics separated from morality," she seems to be differentiating between morality as an abstract set of principles and ethics as a practice.[22] She makes a similar distinction in *Revolution in Poetic Language:* "The *ethics* that develops in the process of negativity's unfolding is not the kind of 'ethics' that consists in obedience to laws" (110). Negativity (a term she takes from Hegel but uses in such a way as to link it to dialogism) is that which "can only produce a subject in process/on trial," in other words, the only kind of subject (as well as the only kind of ethics) possible (111). For Kristeva, ethics is a relational, dialogic *practice* in which one acknowledges both the otherness of the other and the otherness of the self to itself (since we are all, as the title of her latest book suggests, *Étrangers à nous-mêmes*).

She admits that "nothing . . . suggests that a feminine ethics is possible," (185), yet notes that the "reformulation" of contemporary ethics "demands the contribution of women" (185). Kristeva provides her own woman's contribution; in her neologistic "herethics," she may be establishing a maternal if not feminine ethics. Kristeva writes that "herethics is undeath, love" (playing with the pun in French on *a-mort,* undeath, and *amour,* love); herethics is "perhaps no more than that which in life makes bonds, thoughts, and therefore the thought of death, bearable" (185). A mother, too, is she who (or that which) produces life, undeath, as well as exposes and loves the otherness of even ourselves.[23]

This masterful, historico-psychoanalytic text gives birth to another, different text just when it first invokes the terms "the maternal" and "maternality." The first word of the disruptive left column is "FLASH," in both French and English. Since the left column generally weaves and folds associatively rather than progressing linearly or chronologically, it's not obvious what "instant of time" (162) this "flash" is describing. References to "swollen atoms of a bond" and "loving" might indicate this passage concerns the moment of conception, or perhaps the beginnings of fetal development. But perhaps this maternal narrative begins with the flash of light awaiting the newborn in the brightly lit delivery room or from the waiting photographer's flashbulb ("photos of what is not yet visible," perhaps the not-yet-emerged infant), or with a flashback for the mother (162). Kristeva later refers to the "flash that bedazzles me when I confront the abyss between what was mine and is henceforth but irreparably alien" (179).

It's interesting that the first two lyrical, "personal" passages, separated from each other by several pages, include no personal pronouns; the first "my," "I," and even "his" (referring to the fetus) don't occur until the third paragraph; suddenly, gender, identity, and difference are born. Kristeva notes later that "the languages of the great formerly matriarchal civilizations must avoid, do avoid, personal pronouns," relying instead on context, on tones, on a "trans-verbal communication between bodies. ... A woman's discourse, would that be it?" (182) As elsewhere in this essay, her text does not remain such a "woman's discourse."

The two columns do not remain alien to each other; in their dialogue, they often mingle and overlap, echo and anticipate. The speaking mother's milk is first described sensually on the left (171), and her tears at her son's sickness (173); her son's tears have been noted earlier (166). Later, the right column announces that "Milk and tears became the privileged signs of the *Mater Dolorosa* . . . " (173); they are also united in being "the metaphors of non-speech, of a 'semiotics' that linguistic communication does not account for." Both mothers' gift of life and suffering are thus linked to each other, to their sons, and to "the extra-linguistic regions of the unnameable" (174), the semiotic. Notably, death is discussed first on the right ("Neither sex nor death," [165]); Mary is free from death through Assumption or Dormition, as "maternal receptacle —she is transported" (168). The left column's speaker writes, in turn, of the death inherent in birth: "Frozen placenta, live limb of a skeleton, monstrous graft of life on myself, a living dead. Life . . . death . . . undecidable" (168).

Much of Kristeva's recent work has concerned, perhaps deconstructed, metaphysics, faith, and religion—discourses of both love and death. In this essay, the last word in the left column is "death" *(la mort)* followed by ellipses, a sign of the irresolute, of both closure and refusal or lack of closure, of an open space for love *(l'amour)*. The right column follows its invocation of herethics as "undeath" with a request to "let us listen to the *Stabat Mater,*" whose music "swallows up the goddesses and removes their necessity" (185); perhaps both love and death, if not goddesses (or gods), are necessities. Certainly love and death are the master tropes in this essay and intimately related to both maternity and narrative.

The columns themselves die (end) simultaneously (at least in the French text). The right-hand, theoretical/historical column has comprised far more of the essay than the left column, sometimes taking over all or most of a page, while the left column always remains only a partial text, taking up only and always the left side of the page. The dominant symbolic discourse of (the) right seems the master text, interrupted by the repressed "voice" of the semiotic, of what's left.

At times, the abstract, analytical language of the right-hand column penetrates the "personal," usually lyrical, evocative, sensuous language of the left. For example, on the left, Kristeva discusses the Christian Logos, the Jesuits, the Reformation (176–77). Rarely does the columnar "penetration" work the other way.[24] The columns actually begin to sound more and more alike as the essay progresses, but it's the left column that becomes more like the right, rather than vice versa. Earlier invoking "stream of hair, made of ebony, of nectar," (166), the left's last intervention begins "The love of God and for God resides in a gap" (184).

Although it may appear that the symbolic, logocentric discourse is winning out and repressing or mastering the semiotic, given their unequal representation in the essay,[25] I don't believe Kristeva is setting the semiotic and symbolic up as opponents in a battle to the death. Since their relationship is dialogic rather than dialectical, neither must nor can ever conquer the other.[26] As I've noted, Kristeva associates dialectic with struggle and transcendence, while the dialogic remains relational and refuses transcendence ("Word" 88–89). Of course, even the dialogic is susceptible to unequal power relationships, but, at least in principle, it respects alterity rather than seeking to synthesize or vanquish it.

Some commentators believe Kristeva puts the semiotic and symbolic in a dialectical relationship, although they don't necessarily assume that this dialectic implies eventual victory (or at least *Aufhebung*).[27] Other commentators, though, believe that in Kristevan theory, if not in life, either the semiotic or the symbolic gets the upper hand in the dialectic. One can almost divide Kristeva's critics into those who excoriate her for privileging the semiotic and those who do for privileging the symbolic. Smith, for instance, argues that "Kristeva turns her emphasis away from the mutually constraining dialectic between the semiotic and the symbolic, and toward a revindication of a putative priority and primacy of the semiotic" (*Discerning* 126). Judith Butler, though, argues that Kristeva's very theory of the subversive potential of the semiotic is built on an acceptance of the Symbolic as "hegemonic," since paternal law sustains the illusion that the maternal or semiotic is prediscursive and pre-Symbolic; for Butler, there is no "true body beyond the law" (82, 93). Yet, Kristeva acknowledges that "bio-physiological processes" are "already inescapably part of signifying processes" ("System" 28), and thus both symbolic and semiotic.

Certainly, Kristeva has often argued that one cannot refuse the symbolic without becoming psychotic. Yet revolutionary art, the semiotic, and the maternal can push up against and perhaps expand the symbolic's limits. In an interview, Kristeva speaks of a "proper articulation" of mastery and body, symbolic and semiotic, in which "proper" means "that which best fits the specific history of each woman, which best expresses her" ("Two Interviews" 123). Much of her work has been an attempt to think outside of these binary oppositions—male/female, semiotic/symbolic—to transgress or crucify them. But *can* we think outside of them? Kristeva imagines elsewhere the possibility of a time when "the very dichotomy man/woman as an opposition between two rival entities may be understood as belonging to *metaphysics*" ("Women's Time" 209).[28]

Perhaps Kristeva is both using and deconstructing binary oppositions in the very structure of this essay, through the relations between and effects of these two (at least initially so) different columns. The right, analytical column seems to be both about and in the voice of the master, the dominant discourse, patriarchy, in other words, the symbolic order. The left column, seemingly experiential and personal, is both about and in the voice of "misstery," the discourse of the body, the unconscious, the avant-garde, in other words, the semiotic. This text seems to lend itself to such binary analysis. Yet, both "texts" are narratives, neither column does stand alone, and it is the right, "paternal" column that "gives birth to" the left, maternal column. They remain in dialogue; the essay is, quite literally, "double-voiced."

As Jane Gallop sees it, the essay's doubling reflects the status of its speaking subject, "a mother . . . being split between the singleness of the speaking subject (the totalizing 'I') and the doubleness experienced in maternity" (127–28). I don't see even the right column, though, as unified or totalized, since it needs the left column for its "completion."

Nor is it clear, as some commentators simply assume,[29] that the "I" of the left-hand column is Kristeva herself, and that the text is autobiographical, in the usual sense of this term. Does Kristeva's arguable status as a feminist, and unarguable status as the mother of a son, persuade one to read the "personal" text as autobiographical rather than fictive? While Kristeva and most poststructuralists might not see this as a legitimate distinction, it is a philosophical and generic distinction critics often do make (for instance, in even positing "autobiography" and "novel" as distinct genres). We cannot simply assume the speaker is (identical to) the "real" Kristeva; it is at least a fictionalized version of herself or of a poeticized mother's voice, of a mother's discourse.

While commentators like Gallop focus on the speaking subject's production of and relation to this double discourse, I'm also interested in the effects of this discourse on the reader, the reading subject. Kristeva shares Bakhtin's dialogic model of both writing and reading. As she notes in her essay on Bakhtin, "By the very act of narrating, the subject of narration addresses an other, narration is structured in relation to this other." Writing is a "trace of a dialogue with oneself (with another)," and the text is "a dialogue of two discourses," a "coming-and-going movement between subject and other, between writer (W) and reader" ("Word" 74–75). Who is "Stabat Mater's" other and how will she read this doubling text?

The difficulty for the reader is in knowing how to read this dual text—in knowing how to maneuver her eyes in the real activity of reading, but, even more importantly, in knowing how to position herself in relation to the subject-positions that both columns seem to imagine for her.[30]

Should or can we constantly move back and forth between the columns, reading a section, a paragraph, a page of each and then switching to the other? If we do, then *we* experience a kind of vertigo or doubling or even splitting, like a mother and like the speaking subject herself in the essay. This text is, like the maternal body, "the place of a splitting" ("Motherhood According to Giovanni Bellini" 238). The speaking subject may thus reproduce in the reading subject the very tension between sameness and otherness, identification and difference that, in Kristeva's analysis, a mother undergoes.[31] With the two columns, we *experience* as well as *read about* the tension between the Logos and those voices always threatening to disrupt it—the voice of woman as other, the voice of the poet, the voice of the body or the unconscious, the voice of the semiotic.

Yet, a reader's specific relation to and experience of both columns of this challenging text depend on who that reader is — whether a woman, a man, another mother, a woman not a mother, a Christian, a non-Christian, etc. (Kristeva's very name, as well as this essay, invokes Christ, after all.) For those readers not mothers, the discourse *by* the mother may be alien, exotic, spoken by a sort of "native informant" from the land of mothers. For non-Christian readers, the discourse *about* the Virgin Mother may seem merely a description of a quaint or peripheral phenomenon, not a powerful cultural myth or religious symbol.

Perhaps this text's ideal imagined reader would be a heterosexual Christian woman who has borne at least one son and who knows something about theoretical and literary avant-gardes. If one doesn't match this description on any or all counts, then perhaps one becomes the very other, even the other woman, of whom this text speaks. Does this text love or exclude and marginalize such an other? Might this "other reader" decide to read the maternal as metaphorical in order not to be excluded?

Just as love and power are issues in Kristeva's analysis of the Virgin Mary construct, so they are issues in any reading of Kristeva's powerful narratives of childbirth and history, and in any relation to an other.

Narrative itself always implies mastery, even if subversion always awaits in the voices of the semiotic, the transgressive, the unconscious (both the writer's and the reader's). To tell a (fictive or personal) story is to impose order on chaotic experience, to master experience in order to tell about it. To tell a *theoretical* story, to do philosophy, in other words, to narrate ideas, means assuming a position of mastery even more; at least the reader will assume that the theorist, like an analyst or teacher or any narrator, is what Lacan calls "the subject who is supposed to know." Becoming a subject supposed to know requires complicity between the subject and the other. As Ross Chambers puts it, "to tell a story is to exercise power" but power authorized by those "subject to the power" (50). Narrative authority (like dialogism) is both enacted and problematized in Kristeva's text; without being able to master its duelling/dualling voices, can we withdraw our authorization of its narrative or maternal power?[32]

In this unconventional text, perhaps Kristeva is actually being doubly masterful — speaking the master discourse of history and philosophy in the right column, from the position of a subject who *does know*, and speaking the maternal discourse of the body and of gestation and childbirth in the left column, from the position of a subject who also *knows*. Both can be exclusionary textual strategies, excluding on the one hand women and men who are not masters of theoretical discourse and, on the other, women who are not mothers and all men — unless the text *makes* us all mothers metaphorically, as split subjects, or reveals to us that we already are both. As Kristeva notes, "a woman or mother is a conflict — the incarnation of the split of the complete subject, a passion" ("A New Type" 297).

A split essay about splitting (the splitting of the mother and of all subjects), a postmodern limit-text about textual (and human) limits, "Stabat Mater" is, at least in part, a meta-narrative about the possibilities of "mater-narrative" — a narrative about narrative, and about how to tell a mother's story. But can one create a meta-discourse of motherhood or of discourse itself from outside (beyond, *meta*-) the "maternal" or discourse? This is as impossible as trying to locate oneself outside of metaphor to analyze metaphor, as Derrida argues in "White Mythology," or outside of metaphysics or the Symbolic in order to deconstruct them.

Lacan has asserted the "impossibility of a metalanguage," or at least that "no meta-language can be spoken" ("The subversion" 314, 311). But a text, *this* text, can *enact* if not *speak* a meta-language. Perhaps meta-linguistic *effects* can be produced even if messages "about" them are impossibilities. Kristeva notes the dialogic relationship between "representation *by* language and . . . experience *in* language" ("Word" 85). Textual effects and textual meaning may engage in the same dialogic relation that occurs between the semiotic and symbolic. Drucilla Cornell and Adam Thurschwell make a similar point: "Ultimately, the 'truth' of nonidentity can only be shown, not told" (160). Language is the site of nonidentity — of signifier and signified, of subject and object; language is the site of metaphor.

I'd like to suggest that the maternal becomes for Kristeva a metaphor for metaphor itself,[33] which she calls "the economy that modifies language when subject and object of the utterance act muddle their border" ("Throes of Love: The Field of the Metaphor" 268). This definition resembles her description of mother as crossroads being, as she who lives on these very borders. She writes of "motherhood, that mute border" which Bellini (or another artist, like Kristeva?) can provide with a language, "although in doing so, he deprives it of any right to a real existence," but does "accord it a symbolic status" ("Bellini" 249). At the borders between this "real" and "symbolic," in their dialogic relation, lies metaphor, too.

Kristeva locates metaphor in discourse, in "the relationship the speaking subject has with the Other during the utterance act" ("Throes" 274). The Other is "the very space of metaphorical shifting" ("Freud and Love" 38). Metaphoricalness is the "linguistic correlative" of love, "the amatory experience"; they both involve the "dynamics of the crisis and of subjective and discoursive [sic] renewal" ("Throes" 275).

Love and metaphor are also linked to faith: "theological discourse alone, concerned with the One and the relationship of the speaking being to that One — hence with faith — was forced to proceed edge-to-edge along the metaphor" (275). Faith and love both depend on metaphor, and the mother enables and expresses both faith and love. Kristeva sees religious faith (paternal, symbolic) as a transmutation of the (maternal, semiotic) relation to the (archaic) mother: "faith could be described, perhaps rather simplistically, as what can only be called a primary identification with a loving and protective agency. . . . a continuity or fusion with an Other that is no longer substantial and maternal but symbolic and paternal" (*In the Beginning* 24). Psychoanalysis and avantgarde literature, like theology, which, for Kristeva, they now supplant,[34] both proceed by metaphor. As Kristeva puts it, "We are all subjects of the metaphor" (279).

Metaphor is not just a trope of resemblance, but the very condition of language. As Nietzsche puts it, "When we speak of trees, colors, snows, and flowers, we believe we know something about the things themselves, although what we have are just metaphors of things, which do not correspond to the original entities" ("On Truth and Lying" 249). He also writes, "There are no things-in-themselves! . . . Something unconditioned cannot be known: otherwise it would not be unconditioned! Knowing, however, is always a process of 'coming into relation with something . . . ' " (*Will to Power* 64).

All language, like all knowledge, depends on metaphor; thus there can be no viable binary opposition between the metaphorical and the literal. Just as Kristeva seems to deconstruct the notion of the *corps propre* in *Powers of Horror,* and of what I'd call the *maternelle propre* in "Stabat Mater" and other sites, so Derrida (in "White Mythology") and Nietzsche deconstruct the notion of a *sens propre.* The "clean and proper body" that tries to expel the abject while being constituted by it is like the dream of a "proper" (selfsame, self-present, nonmetaphorical) language. In Kristeva, the maternal and metaphor itself reveal the impossibility of the "proper," and the possibility of transgression.

"Metaphor" (from the Greek, *metapherein,* to transfer, to carry or bear beyond) comes from the same root as "to bear children," to give birth to. It is also etymologically related to "transgress" (to step across). Metaphor, transgression, and the maternal involve relation to the other and the crossing of boundaries, especially those of the proper. Metaphor, like the split subject (and like the maternal), is always elsewhere, always other to itself. The otherness of metaphor is (like) the otherness of all language and the otherness of both the Other and the subject.

To link the maternal, if not Woman, to metaphor in this way is thus to place the maternal into the very womb of language, rather than in its margins, or outside its orbit (if such a position were imaginable). Certainly, Kristeva has often linked the "feminine" and the unnameable or unrepresentable in problematic ways. In "Stabat Mater," she writes of the "unnameable that one imagines as femininity, non-language, or body" (162) (yet note the key use of "imagines"). Domna Stanton argues that Kristeva's use of the maternal metaphor is ontotheological and runs the risk of revalorizing the phallogocentric vision of woman as the unrepresentable other, as lack.[35] But, unlike Stanton, I don't believe metaphor solely functions "to provide for a missing term, to say what lacks, is absent"; woman is not associated with metaphor only if "*la différence féminine* [is] defined as absence" (Stanton 163). Metaphor is not less than meaning nor its mere supplement. Metaphor is dialogic, relational; it, like "the other," is inevitable.

Kristeva sees the "space of fundamental unrepresentability" as "a primal scene where genitality dissolves sexual identification beyond their [the mother and father's] given difference" ("Bellini" 249). The semiotic *chora* may be, not the domain of the "feminine," but the very site of this abolition of sexual difference—unrepresentable and perhaps unthinkable (like God? like negativity? like metaphor? like a non-metaphoric language? like the other/Other?).

Yet, to read Kristeva's use of the maternal as more metaphorical than biological presents at least the same problems that many feminists find in separating Lacan's notion of the phallus from the actual penis. Can metaphors be severed from their roots? For Lacan, "the phallus" becomes the prime signifier, the signifier of signification itself.[36] Although Stanton and other critics legitimately worry about using "the mother" (or "woman") as the signifier of the impossibility of meaning or of that which resists signification, "the mother" can be seen instead as a signifier of the possibility of contingent, temporary, dialogic meanings.

Perhaps, in her typically non-agonistic (dialogic?) revision of Lacan, Kristeva is suggesting that psychoanalysis can replace "the phallus" with the "maternal" as the signifier of signification. The maternal doesn't avoid the loss castration and entry into the symbolic require. But at least the maternal refers to a process rather than (arguably) a specific bodily organ, and it doesn't pose as unitary. Perhaps the maternal and language are homologous in existing at "the threshold of culture and nature," in being "WORD FLESH" ("Stabat" 182, 162). As Kristeva puts it, "A mother is a continuous separation, a division of the very flesh. And consequently a division of language" ("Stabat" 178).

But mothers clearly aren't only philosophemes nor metaphors — even of metaphor or language itself. The "maternal" as metaphor cannot float free of its connection to the real biological phenomenon of (some) actual women bearing actual children. Feminist critics debate whether Kristeva essentializes women by a glorification of the maternal — reinstating old stereotypes and social obligations — or effaces real women, their bodies, their differences.[37] I think Kristeva (barely) skirts both dangers.

As Gallop argues, "it is a stultifying reduction to subsume femininity into the category of maternity. But it is an opposite and perhaps even equally defensive reduction to believe in some simple separation of the two categories" (116). Although Kristeva has been accused of equating femininity and the maternal, she writes, in "Stabat Mater," of the "resorption of femininity within the Maternal" which "is specific to many civilizations," but which Christianity "brings . . . to its peak"; she calls this a "masculine appropriation" produced by either primary narcissism or sublimation (163). I think it safe to say that Kristeva doesn't believe that the feminine and the maternal should be conflated, even if historically they have been so conflated. She also suggests that "one needs to listen, more carefully than ever, to what mothers are saying today, through their economic difficulties . . . , their discomforts, joys, angers . . . " ("Stabat" 179).

In Kristeva's texts, the maternal is linked to, but not equated with, the actual experiences — varied and complex — of actual mothers and actual women, but it is available to others, too. Perhaps there's something to be gained by (plural) theories or metaphors of the maternal that allow mothers, child-free women, and even men to *become* (rather than *be*) "maternal." Since discourse (especially theoretical discourse) is irremediably metaphorical, we need better (or at least different) metaphors; why not dethrone the phallus, even if the maternal is crowned only transitionally?[38]

Kristeva does link the pre-Oedipal, prelinguistic realm of the semiotic to the maternal, to what she, following Plato in his *Timaeus*, calls, metaphorically, the *chora:* "an ancient, mobile, unstable receptacle, prior to the One, to the father, and even to the syllable, metaphorically suggesting something nourishing and maternal" (*In the Beginning* 5). The chora seems to be a potential, mobile, nonspatial space of energy, of *"pulsions"* (*pulsion* is the Lacanian French translation of Freud's term *Trieb*, drive or instinct), metaphorically womblike.

Yet, the pre-Oedipal "archaic mother" with which both the *chora* and the semiotic are associated includes or transcends both masculine and feminine; as Toril Moi notes, "the opposition between feminine and masculine does not exist in pre-Oedipality" (165). In "Freud and Love: Treatment and Its Discontents," Kristeva discusses Freud's theory of the "father in individual prehistory," with whom the subject identifies pre-Oedipally; she suggests that, "because there is no awareness of sexual difference during that period . . . , such a 'father' is the same as 'both parents' " (26).

In Kristeva's analysis, the semiotic is linked to the maternal rather than the feminine, but this maternal semiotic is available to both males and females, and always accompanies and threatens the symbolic.[39] Certainly, Kristeva has argued that the semiotic is as much the site of the avant-garde artist as of the mother, so it can only be maternal functionally or metaphorically. Art, or at least revolutionary art, is a "semiotization of the symbolic" representing "the flow of jouissance into language" (*Revolution* 79).[40] For Kristeva, a male avant-garde writer like Joyce or Burroughs or Sollers is as semiotic as a mother (or probably more so). In fact, as Stanton, Jardine, and Grosz, among others, have noted, Kristeva has more often written about male avant-garde writers than about mothers or even women, especially women writers. "Stabat Mater" is one of the few texts in which Kristeva writes about not only the virgin mother but also a woman writer; narcissistically, perhaps, that woman is a fictionalized version of herself.

As Jane Gallop notes, "The semiotic is the locus of force, revolution and art in Kristeva's work . . . " (124). In "Stabat Mater" and other texts, Kristeva has argued for the transformative potential of transgressive discourses — discourses of the semiotic, the avant-garde, the un-conscious. The claim that literature or language *can* transform the world has been challenged as well as defended by countless critics and theo-rists, not only those who write about Kristeva. Moi, for instance, argues that Kristeva seems to assume that "the disruption of the subject" in avant-garde texts "prefigures or parallels revolutionary disruptions of society," but that "her only argument in support of this contention is the rather lame one of comparison or homology." Moi asserts that, fi-nally, "Kristeva is unable to account for the relations between the sub-ject and society" (171). Yet, since the Kristevan subject is created in and through language, at the place where word and flesh meet (*In the Begin-ning* 6), and since language is a social practice, how can the subject and the social be severed? Although not all recent Kristevan texts provide "materialist analysis of social relations" (Moi 171), all her theories of the speaking subject are, finally, social.

Love, language, art, the maternal, faith, and ethics are, after all, social relations, broadly defined — relations to the other. Like metaphor and the dialogic, they exist on the thresholds between the subject and the other. Analysis of individual subjects' relations to others and to themselves cannot replace broader sociopolitical analysis (of groups, of power relations, of larger discursive formations), but both types of analysis have a legitimate place in the world of theory.

Kristeva believes, and I agree, "that there can be no socio-political transformation without a transformation of subjects: in other words, in our relationship to social constraints, to pleasure, and more deeply, to language" ("Woman can never" 141). Such transformation of subjects (and of their relations to others) is a necessary but not sufficient condi-tion for genuine socio-political change. Foucault, a more political and less psychoanalytic observer, makes a similar point: "We have to pro-mote new forms of subjectivity through the refusal of this kind of indi-viduality which has been imposed on us for several centuries" ("Sub-ject and Power" 216). Kristeva, too, talks about the power of refusal, of negativity, of rejection, in fact asserting "that a feminist practice can only be negative, at odds with what already exists" ("Woman can never" 137).[41]

Kristeva has argued that "the moment of transgression is the key moment in practice" and that it relies on a "transgression of the unity proper to the transcendental ego" or subject. The split subject — at the crossroads of language and the unconscious, the symbolic and the semiotic, word and flesh — is positioned to "get pleasure from . . . , re-new . . . , even endanger" the sociosymbolic system ("System" 29, 30).

The mother, the artist, the speaking and reading subjects of "Stabat Mater" are all positioned at these crossroads. This essay is perhaps Utopian in implying that love, maternity (both literal and metaphorical), and art — as metaphorical, dialogic practices — can enable subjects to use, subvert, and renew the sociosymbolic order. Utopia, like the *chora*, may be no-place, yet one can seek the impossible.

## NOTES

1. An earlier version of this paper was presented at the 1990 Conference on Narrative (April, New Orleans). I'd like to thank the National Endowment for the Humanities for enabling my participation in a 1989 Summer Seminar on Postmodernism, and Ihab Hassan for directing that seminar, in which I first began to work on Kristeva's recent texts. I'd also like to thank two former students, Mick Markham and Kathleen Maloney, for first getting me to read "Stabat Mater" when they chose to write papers on it. And I'd especially like to thank Diane Jonte-Pace both for enlightening conversations about Kristeva and psychoanalysis and for her suggestions on this paper.

2. As Derrida notes, there is no nonmetaphoric language with which to describe or get beyond or master metaphor; "metaphor" itself is a metaphor ("White Mythology," esp. 219–220).

3. Moi, Roudiez ("Introduction," *Desire in Language*), and other commentators refer to Kristeva's arrival in Paris in 1966, but Kristeva writes of attending midnight mass at Notre Dame at Christmas in 1965 ("My Memory's Hyperbole" 263).

4. In the tone of a sharply disappointed former fan, Smith presents in this essay one of the most sustained attacks on Kristeva's recent work. In particular, he criticizes her turn away from her former materialism to a (bourgeois, liberal) individualism, her antifeminism and anti-Marxism, her appreciation of the United States, her privileging of literary texts and individual psyches as the primary loci of possible change or transgression, etc. In *Discerning the Subject*, he presents a more balanced account, arguing that her earlier work is more valuable than her later. More sympathetic critiques of the recent turns in Kristeva's work are provided, for example, by Jacqueline Rose, who finds an "overall consistency of Kristeva's project" ("Julia Kristeva: Take Two" 163), and Toril Moi *(Sexual/Textual Politics)*; both, however, believe that at least some elements of Kristeva's work—old and new—have value for feminist theorists, in particular. Suzanne Clark provides a valuable contextualizing assessment of Kristeva's recent work. Alice Jardine observes that there are "three Kristevas— . . . the Kristevas of the 1960s, 70s and 80s" with "more Kristevas to come" ("Opaque" 106). Kristeva herself notes some readers' "tendency to see decided reversals" in her

work, as its "dominant concerns" have changed. Yet, as she notes, " 'Semantic materialism' may have been overtaken by the 'subject on trial,' but it was never eclipsed" ("My Memory's Hyperbole" 269).

5. For critiques of Kristeva's relation to feminism and/or politics, see Grosz, Rose, Stanton, Moi, Gallop, Smith, and Butler. New work critical of Kristeva seems to be appearing daily.

6. Jones writes: "Kristeva began by raising important issues of subjectivity in culture, but she has ended up with escape routes that are especially unconsoling for women. Religion and romantic love have not been alternatives to women's subordination; they have been the ideologies through which that subordination was lived" (70).

Kristeva's complex relations to religion/religious discourse are, of course, the subject of this book. Clark provides a useful frame of reference for understanding Kristeva's interest in religion, pointing out that "unlike American intellectuals, she writes about religion in the context of a thoroughly secular environment, and a past experience in Bulgaria where the church was a source of possible freedom from totalitarian authority" ("Julia Kristeva and the Feminine Subject" 2). I might add that religious discourse becomes a real repressed other in a Communist state that, like Bulgaria when Kristeva lived there, strictly regulated religion (although "freedom of conscience" was guaranteed in the constitution). Kristeva refers to being raised in a "family of believers" and often writes about Catholicism (*In the Beginning* 23); Leon Roudiez says "she received her early schooling from French nuns" ("Introduction" to *Desire in Language* 1). I infer from this and other evidence that Kristeva was raised in the Roman Catholic rather than the Orthodox Church (although she also refers to kneeling, as an adolescent, before an icon of the Virgin, contemplating its "Byzantine iconography" [*In the Beginning* 23]). Roman Catholics were a very small minority in Bulgaria; most believers were Orthodox. In 1948, the Communist government confiscated all Catholic schools and institutions and banished all religious who were not Bulgarians ("Bulgaria"; see also Crampton, esp. 171–174). Since Kristeva would have been only seven at that time, I'm curious about how (secretly, illegally, abroad?) she could have been schooled by French nuns.

7. Kristeva notes this change herself in the preface to *Desire in Language:* "The starker style, tending toward a kind of formalization, of the earlier essays, changes progressively as a psychoanalytic trend is accentuated (as well as interest in literary and artistic practices), making way for a more personal style. And yet, this does not go so far as identifying theoretical discourse with that of art— causing theory to be written as literary or para-literary fiction" (ix).

8. Stanton presents a particularly lucid critique of the essentialism and risks of the maternal metaphor in Kristeva, Cixous, and Irigary. Grosz argues that, for Kristeva, "maternity is not the action of a *woman*," for Woman is an essentialist and nonexistent category (80); Grosz does go on to argue that in

Kristeva, maternity, rather than the female or feminine, becomes both essentialist and biologist. Moi argues that Kristeva is neither essentialist nor biologist (163–167). See also Rose and Butler.

9. It's interesting to note that the hymn "Stabat Mater" is also mentioned in Kristeva's husband Philippe Sollers' novel *H*, about which she's written in "The Novel as Polylogue," and in James Joyce's *Ulysses*, in the midst of Molly's soliloquy—a text with a rhythm much like Kristeva's in the left column of her "Stabat." Although I haven't been able to trace them yet, I suspect that a few neologistic English phrases in the French text of "Stabat" come from Joyce. Kristeva often discusses both Sollers and Joyce as representatives of transgressive, avant-garde literature.

10. The intertextual space in which to situate such a two-column essay would broadly include the whole tradition of textual/scriptural commentary, with glosses written in the margins (although these glosses would usually be on others' texts rather than one's own, and neither of Kristeva's columns is reducible to gloss). More specific avant-garde theoretical precursors might include Derrida's *Glas* (1974), as well as his initially dual-column "The Double Session" — itself playing with Mallarmé's typographically experimental *Mimique* and a commentary on that text by Sollers. [See also his "Tympan" in *Margins of Philosophy*—Ed.] This "essay" was published in Kristeva's and Sollers' *Tel Quel* in 1970 (and later included in *Dissemination*). Mallarmé's "Un coup de dés" (which Kristeva discusses in *Revolution in Poetic Language*), also transgresses the usual rules of typography, as do many of Sollers' literary works. Paul Valéry's *Leonardo* (1894; in his *Collected Works*) uses two columns; the left is the main text while the right provides afterthoughts and elaborations on the ideas in the left. Valéry's text thus transgresses temporal boundaries as well as spatial ones. (I'm indebted to Carolyn Grassi for pointing out Valéry's text to me.) As Barbara Johnson notes in her "Translator's Introduction" to *Dissemination*, such typographical play reveals "that an effort is being made to call the reader's attention to the syntactical function of spacing in the act of reading" and produces "one textual fold too many or too few to be accounted for by a reading that would seek only the text's 'message' or 'meaning' " (xxviii).

11. Alice Jardine notes that in its use in the United States, "postmodern" "perhaps most accurately corresponds to what the French name *la modernité* . . . : those writing self-consciously from within the (intellectual, scientific, philosophical, religious, literary) *epistemological crisis* specific to the postwar period" ("Opaque" 98). Kristeva uses the terms "modernity," "modern," or "avant-garde" far more often than "postmodern," but these terms all have a strong family resemblance.

12. Cornell and Thurschwell insightfully discuss this and other significant differences between Lacanian and Kristevan psychoanalytic theory.

13. Kristeva asserts the "founding status" of language, in, among other places, *Powers of Horror* (37). In spite of the antimetaphysical, antifoundationalist claims of much poststructuralist theory, language often becomes foundational.

14. Suzanne Clark notes the influence of Bakhtinian dialogism particularly on Kristeva's concept of subjectivity, in which it is "the dialogic which constitutes the subject." Clark also notes that this dialogic "is not an intersubjectivity of autonomous entities, but an intertextuality" (4).

15. Bakhtin makes a similar distinction between dialogue and dialectics: "Take a dialogue and remove the voices . . . , remove the intonations . . . cram everything into one abstract consciousness—and that's how you get dialectics" ("From Notes" 147).

16. Note the appropriately conditional "if" with which the essay begins. Lacan, too, is fond of beginning his sentences with "if."

17. Although some of Kristeva's critics believe that her interest in religious discourse signaled and accompanied the end of her interest in the political, even here, in examining a religious "construct," Kristeva analyzes social, political, historical, as well as psychoanalytic elements. In *In the Beginning Was Love*, Kristeva also looks at sociopolitical dimensions of Mary's virginity, noting that the "proscription of female sexuality" required "generous compensation in the form of praise of motherhood and its narcissistic rewards"; that proscription could only be lifted recently because of "advances in contraceptive technique" (43).

18. Cf. Rose, esp. 154–157.

19. This homology between mothers and crucifixion takes a further twist when Kristeva writes of abjection, which she associates with the maternal: "Abjection is a resurrection that has gone through death (of the ego). It is an alchemy that transforms death drive into a start of life, of new signifiance" (*Powers of Horror* 15). The maternal association with love, life, and death is also explored below.

20. As Rose notes, the very "act of differentiation-recognition of the other leads—if not to violence—then at least, and of necessity, to psychic pain" (160).

21. Perhaps Freud could not really theorize about that which — unlike castration anxiety, Oedipal rivalry, and dreams, but like "femininity" itself—he had never experienced.

22. In his essay on Kristevan ethics (in this volume), David Fisher makes a similar distinction between an ethics based on principle and one based on context.

23. Kristeva, of course, does not mean to suggest that all mothers are inherently ethical, in their relations to others or even to their own children, nor that they are incapable of infanticide and hate. Perhaps here the maternal becomes an exemplary metaphor for a particular ethical practice.

24. The right column's final call to us to listen to the music of the *Stabat Mater* is an arguably "semiotic" thing to do.

25. The semiotic and symbolic are not equally susceptible to representation, in any event.

26. Rose makes a similar point, calling their relationship "a 'dynamic,' " and arguing that in spite of "the apparent dualism of that semiotic/symbolic division, there is therefore no strict demarcation between them" (146).

27. For instance, Grosz writes that "Kristeva conceives of their [the symbolic and semiotic's] interaction as a dialectic, a confrontation between contradictory forces which enables change to occur" (49).

28. One major division among feminist theorists concerns, precisely, whether this would be a desirable time, this (Utopian?) time beyond sexual differentiation. Kristeva herself suggests in "Stabat Mater" the possibility of "an acknowledgement of what is irreducible, of the irreconcilable interest of both sexes in asserting their differences, in the quest of each one—and of women, after all—for an appropriate fulfillment" (184).

29. For instance, Martha Reineke writes that the left-hand column provides "poetic reflections on the birth and development of Kristeva's own son" in the "words of Kristeva the mother" (457).

30. Father Walter J. Ong notes that "The Writer's Audience Is Always a Fiction." Peter J. Rabinowitz goes further in his analysis, asserting four possible audiences of a fictional text: actual, authorial, narrative, and "*ideal narrative audience*—ideal, that is, from the narrator's point of view" (134). The authorial audience is the one an author "designs his work rhetorically for" by making assumptions about these "readers' beliefs, knowledge, and familiarity with conventions" (126). Although, in "Stabat Mater" the "narrator" and "author" are difficult to differentiate, the text certainly exists in relation to a posited or imagined audience. The work on audience, reception, and reader-response theory is too vast to cite here, but relevant to my analysis.

31. Reineke makes a similar point: "the reader, carried away by Kristeva's writing, arrives at an unnameable space at the limits of the two discourses" (457).

32. Yet, as Nietzsche notes, "the act of interpreting" is itself "a form of the Will to Power . . . a passion" (*Will to Power* 65). Again, reader and writer are both in dialogic interaction, if not agonistic struggle, as dual interpreters and thus makers of the text.

33. I say "*a* metaphor," since, as Derrida notes, there cannot be one metaphor of metaphor ("White Mythology," esp. 268).

34. For example, she writes in *Powers of Horror* that "contemporary literature . . . when it is written as the language, possible at last, of that impossible constituted either by a-subjectivity or by non-objectivity, propounds . . . a sublimation of abjection. Thus it becomes a substitute for the role formerly played by the sacred, at the limits of social and subjective identity. But we are dealing here with a sublimation without consecration" (26). She also sees "psychoanalysis as the lay version, the only one, of the speaking being's quest for truth that religion symbolizes for certain of my contemporaries and friends" ("My Memory's Hyperbole" 267). In numerous places, she makes similar claims that psychoanalytic and literary discourse have replaced theological discourse in our time.

35. As opposed to Stanton, who criticizes Kristeva's use of the maternal metaphor, but believes Kristeva sees metaphor as a paternal function (161), I posit metaphor itself as maternal in Kristeva. Stanton cites a passage in *Powers of Horror*, in which Kristeva is discussing Lacan's view of metaphor as condensation, seen as a "paternal function" whereby the heterogeneous is made unitary. It's not clear whether Kristeva is arguing for this connection between "condensation, metaphoricalness, and more strongly yet, paternal function," or revealing it in Lacan and Freud, whom she is discussing (53). As I've tried to show, Kristeva's texts allow for a reading of metaphor as maternal. Perhaps in metaphor, like the semiotic (see below), differences — including sexual — are abolished.

36. See Lacan's "The signification of the phallus," 281–291. For a discussion of feminist issues in regard to separating the phallus from the penis, see Gallop, esp. 95–101. Gallop argues that "the signifier 'phallus' functions in distinction from 'penis,' but it must also always refer to 'penis' " (96).

37. For instance, Grosz believes that, as with Kristeva's "understanding of femininity, maternity is not the action of a *woman*, of women." Grosz feels that "Kristeva's resistance to attributing *any* female identity to maternity becomes ludicrous, in view of her willingness to describe maternity in biological and physiological terms" (80–81). On essentialism, see also note 8 above.

38. Stanton makes a similar point, noting "the importance of an initial counter-valorization of the maternal-feminine as a negation/subversion of paternal hierarchies, . . . an enabling mythology. But the moment the maternal emerges as a new dominance, it must be put into question before it congeals as feminine essence, as unchanging in-difference" (174).

39. It's unclear what happens, though, to those who are neither artists nor mothers; are they doomed merely to replicate and maintain the symbolic order?

40. Religious faith, too, requires this dialogic relation between the semiotic (maternal) and the symbolic (paternal). So the Christian assertion of the originary status of the Word required a "compensation" in the notion of a "maternal receptacle" in "the virginal fantasy" of Mary ("Stabat" 175–76). Kristeva writes that "fusion with God . . . is more semiotic than symbolic . . . " (*In the Beginning* 25). She argues that faith requires "this 'semiotic' leap toward the other, this primary identfication [sic] with the primitive parental poles close to the maternal container . . . " (26). But unlike religion, which requires the sacrifice of (maternal) jouissance in order to maintain the symbolic order, art introduces jouissance. Faith, like psychotic overidentification with the maternal semiotic, seems to be a state to be gotten beyond; Kristeva believes that "the experience of psychoanalysis can lead to renunciation of faith with clear understanding" (26).

41. As Grosz notes, Kristeva "invokes woman and femininity as a metaphor for a more general and diffuse struggle against identity per se. In this respect her work remains close to Derrida" (65). In addition to her Derridean refusal of "feminine" identity and her deconstruction of gender oppositions (see Cornell and Thurschwell), Kristeva may be Foucauldian in suggesting a refusal of historically constructed identities. She may hold out more optimistic transformative possibilities, though, than Foucault, in suggesting love and ethical practice as positive gestures following this refusal.

## INTER-TEXT 2

The heart of this essay is its detailed reading of "Stabat Mater," its form and style as well as its ideas. But the richness of the discussion comes also from the scope of the intertextuality in which that reading is set: feminist critics of Kristeva, biographical information, Bakhtin's dialogism, Derrida, among others. "Stabat Mater," with its two-column text, is itself an intertextuality, a dialogism. Self-scission and interior alterity, issues important throughout Kristeva's work, are here articulated in a meditation on the emergence of the other within the own body, mirrored in the self-scission of the text. Thus where Jonte-Pace addresses the question of mother as other, for this essay the question is of mother as self, or rather of subject as mother.

Edelstein has brought together a number of criticisms of Kristeva's work, several of which focus on the issue of whether the maternal is an appropriate identification of the feminine. Some of these critics seem to suppose that Kristeva intends her text to set out a normative model of female identity (as maternal). Edelstein resists the strong forms of this adversarial reading, preferring to treat the maternal as metaphor — as metaphor of the feminine [of the human?], and as metaphor of metaphor itself. She worries, though, about the biological, material import of this metaphor, "its connection to the real biological phenomenon of (some) actual women bearing actual children." She judges that Kristeva (barely) skirts the dangers of this literal connection. Some of us would emphasize the fact that materiality is integral to metaphor (and vice versa?), that "mother" as metaphor necessarily does invoke actual women bearing actual children. The question, perhaps, is whether Kristeva's view is to be distinguished from essentialism by softening that invocation or by a firm recognition that, indeed, some women, and only women, are mothers, and that therefore the terms "woman" and "mother" must be thought in some sort of interplay. But the key point is that Kristeva does not propose the category of motherhood as an essential structure, or a defining metaphor, of feminine identity. (Both the question of how to read the Kristevan text and that of the nature of metaphor are at stake here.)

The splitting of Kristeva's text into two columns has provoked a lot of discussion. Edelstein recognizes its suggestion of the separation of the other within, in conception, and of the separation of birth itself. She notes the more personal character of the left column, against the more formal discourse of the right — possibly the woman's discourse of maternity contrasted with the paternal discourse? Or is the difference to be understood as a contrast of the semiotic and the symbolic? Though Edelstein does not explicitly adopt the latter interpretation, she does give it considerable attention. But is not the symbolic, in a Lacanian and Kristevan sense, the realm of discourse in general, in its public meanings and forms? Both columns are then necessarily symbolic; neither is primarily dominated by the sounds, rhythms, somatic differences that mark the semiotic realm. Indeed, for Kristeva there seems not to be a semiotic discourse differentiated from the symbolic by its content; her "revolution in poetic language" appears to consist in recognizing the somatic, pre-Oedipal, presymbolic function of the poetic, of sound and rhythm and form, as overdeterminations of the symbolic discourse. These poetic, somatic, disruptive overdeterminations are not characteristic of Kristeva's left column, which, taken in itself, does not appear avant-garde or experimental, or characterized by these specific features she has identified as the presence of the semiotic in discourse.

The question is more than a matter of detail. If Lacan is right that the symbolic order is structurally, necessarily, a paternal, phallic order, and if Kristeva is right about the archaic maternal foundations of the semiotic (David Fisher's essay explores this in most detail; it also figures in Crownfield and Reineke), then the problem of women's discourse appears to lie beyond the reach of an *écriture* that simply thematizes a feminine content. If the semiotic is not a content of discourse but a structure of its embodiment, then disruption, practice, pluralization are necessary to a feminine discourse. (From this point of view it is not the left column of "Stabat Mater" that is semiotic, but the split text "as a whole.")

The essay includes an extended consideration of the question of metaphor. Edelstein associates metaphor with the non-identity of signifier and signified (the essence of signification) and with the relation of the speaking subject to the other in the act of utterance. As such it is the very condition of language, so there can be no binary opposition of metaphoric to literal, no *sens propre*. Metaphor is transgression, crossing of boundaries, in the very womb of language. It is dialogical, relational. The maternal is not only a metaphor in Kristeva's text as Edelstein reads it but is the metaphor of metaphor itself, in that non-identity, relation-

in-act, transgression, are the dynamic of both the maternal and the metaphoric. Not castration, as in Lacan, but self-differentiation of the flesh
is the matrix of language.

There are a nest of interesting issues here. The homology of
mother and metaphor is suggestive. It does appear to appeal to the kind
of association of mother with other, with absence, that Jonte-Pace
wishes to disestablish, though Edelstein is aware of this problem and
wishes to avoid it (as her discussion of Stanton indicates). In addition,
at the core of poststructuralist discussions of linguistic signification is
the fact that the sign is the absence of the object; how can one homolo-
gize signification and mother without homologizing mother and absence, with all the disadvantages Jonte-Pace has identified? Also, what
is the relation, in figuring metaphor, between the maternal as *chora*, as
the matrix of the semiotic in infantile prehistory, and the maternal as the
self-division of the (mother's) flesh, as articulated in "Stabat Mater"?
Does Edelstein wind up homologizing the semiotic to the former and
the symbolic to the latter? To supplement, or replace, or dialectically
counter, the phallic model of signification by a maternal one is an interesting strategy. Is it Kristeva's? Can it work? Or will we then wind up
homologizing the maternal to the phallic, reducing self-division to castration, and reinstating the Lacanian Name of the Father in the maternal
womb itself?

Another important theme of Edelstein's essay, already involved in
the discussion of metaphor, is the question of how to read a text, this
text. She raises questions of authorial intention, of Kristeva as a pur-
ported "subject supposed to know." She questions whether the ideal
reader must not be a heterosexual Christian woman who has borne a
son and who knows about literary theory. Narrative, she holds, always
implies mastery. Perhaps, she says, the split form of the Kristevan text
represents a double mastery: on the right, the master discourse of theory and history, and on the left the mastery of the masters in a text of
one who experientially knows what the master can not know.

Edelstein's use of Lacan's phrase, "the subject who is supposed to
know," may be the key to this problematic. For Lacan, the phrase des-
ignates the position into which the analyzand locates the analyst, with
the result that the conversation takes place between the imaginary ego
of the analyzand (constituted by the reflection given in the gaze and address of the other) and the transferential, imaginary place in which the
analyst is located by this reflection. It is artificial and fictitious, it is constructed by the analyzand, the construction is dominated by the disturbance the analysis is supposed to treat, and it is necessary to bring it to

clarity and deconstruct it in order for the analysis to be successful. Applying these considerations to Edelstein's use of the phrase would suggest that the authorial position as mastery is a fictive construction of the reader, a distortion of the communication, a dysfunctional process that needs to be deconstructed.

Edelstein's image of the ideal reader of "Stabat Mater" as a heterosexual Christian mother of a son would then reflect not a position constructed by an author, but the imaginary place in which the reader locates him/herself by identifying with the text as a mirror, by constructing oneself as "what mother wants." Edelstein moves beyond this position by electing to construe the text as positioning the reader only metaphorically in the situation of the mother of a son. What makes this work is not so much the appeal to metaphor, which is going to be difficult if metaphor has the centrality Edelstein elsewhere gives it, but her notion of inventing the "other reader" who decides how to read the text. Perhaps, indeed, for any text there is only an "other reader" who cannot occupy the imaginary position of the ideal reader but must elect, must construe, must acknowledge both identities and differences with what appears in the reading. Edelstein makes this move, but she does not identify it as the very nature of reading a text.

# 3

# THE SUBLIMATION OF NARCISSISM IN CHRISTIAN LOVE AND FAITH

## David R. Crownfield

*David Crownfield's essay examines Kristeva's account of the construction of self in its relation to narcissism and its application to the interpretation of Christianity. He finds that Kristeva's discourse is unable to sustain a difference between religion's illusion and its own disillusion, and poses the question whether Christianity, dis-illusioned, fictive, erotic, may still have some playing space in our contemporary world.*

Freud regarded love as a sort of madness founded in narcissism. The individual idealizes and inflates the other either on the basis of the essentially autoerotic pleasure of which the other is the instrument, or on the basis of an identification with the other who thus represents an inflation and idealization of myself. Freud does not give a detailed account of the process by which the narcissism underlying these idealizations comes into being, though he does call it "something added . . . a new psychical action" ("On Narcissism," *Standard Edition* 14:77). In *Tales of Love* Julia Kristeva addresses this issue, with the aid of some concepts of Jacques Lacan.

In her view, the foundation for narcissism lies in the initial disturbance of the mother-child dyad by the presence of the third party. This is not, at this level, an Oedipal, sexual rivalry, but the primordial recognition that there is an other to mother. There is somebody, and at the same time I am a collage of sensations, an invisible, a gap or nothingness having no solid place in the mother-world in which the other appears. What Kristeva calls the zero degree of subjectivity is my originary imagining of myself as the somebody, an imagining that takes the form of a sort of rudimentary pattern-replication, or mimicry of the other. The hole, the nothing, is covered over, masked, fictively replaced by this imagined somebody that begins to be my self (*Tales of Love* 24 – 31).

This masking is not without cost. The covering is lined with terror and rage, at mother, at the other, at my fictive self, at the gap. The essentially triadic structure of self (mother, other and gap) is always on the brink of collapse into a dyad: either a would-be restitution of the original mother-child dyad, but now in support of a self, a somebody, a consciousness of difference, a panic of exclusivity (narcissism in a familiar sense); or else an imaginary nihilation of mother, a dyad with the other, a degradation and abhorrence of the maternal (abjection). In either case, the negation of the third is intensified by its instability: the foundation on which the negation stands, the self that would deny the other, is constituted in the triadic relation it seeks to refuse and is thus always threatened by its own originary dynamics (41 – 45).

The situation is complicated by the Oedipal drama. Already when that scene opens, there is the problem of the third party. My self is already an imaginary substitution of the image of the other for the gap in being that I am (26 – 33). This substitution is already a mimicry, a mimicry of the sounds as well as the gestures of the third party (24 – 26). With the emergence of sexuality, the problem of the third party becomes specifically the question, "What does mother want?" (i.e., how can I constitute myself as being/having what mother wants? [34, 40]). Following Freud and Lacan, Kristeva uses the symbol of the phallus to represent what mother wants. The issue here is not literally that of the penis, but of the whole unnameable and ungraspable dynamics of mother's desire for what I am not—what I still am not even in my imaginary selfhood. The gap has reappeared even in my imaginary being (42f).

The child's imitation of the third party is a sort of ur-metaphor. Entry into the other's discourse—acquisition of language—functions both as mimicry and as substitution of discourse for possession. It is in the world of discourse that I must come to terms with desire and lack, with mother's desire for the other, with the other's barring me from possession. Language, the law of the father, the "no" of the father, becomes the scene of displacement and substitution and denial of desire, the substitute for the phallus, the covering of the gap, the mimicry of being (35 – 38). In the process, our own genitality becomes an integral part of the signifying system, marking and classifying our identification with mother or with father, barring a daughter from mother's having, a son from having mother, marking each one's symbolic castration as either the fate of one's anatomy (for a daughter) or as a failure to live up to one's anatomy (for a son) (Lacan, *Écrits: A Selection* 152).

For Freud, narcissism is an investment of erotic energy in the ego rather than in objects. In Kristeva's analysis, it is investment in the symbolic representation of the imaginary self, a collapsing of the triadic foundation of selfhood into a dyad, a fundamental denial of otherness. In the madness of love, I transfer to the loved one the imaginary idealization on which my own selfhood is founded, and I find in the other's love a quasi-parental affirmation and support for my imaginary being. In any case, the problem of imaginary selfhood and of the instability of its triadic foundation requires in general what she calls a narcissan project. The specific forms of this project that collapse the triad into an imaginary dyad are what she calls narcissism in the strict sense (45 – 47).[1]

This process is articulated in a symbolic system that is historically specific. In the history of the West, for example, there have developed determinate ideas of self, other, love, meaning, and God that have configured and reinforced specific forms of symbolization of self, that have enabled the sublimation of rage and terror, and that have supported the triadic relationality or favored its collapse into a dyadic narcissism. *Tales of Love* contains a series of studies of literary and religious texts articulating specific economies of narcissism and relationality. Plotinus, for example, Kristeva sees as articulating an ideal for selfhood that is fundamentally dyadic, fundamentally narcissistic, in its contemplation of the ideal other that is at the same time its own being. Symbolically sublimated, this dyadic self is viable; but it lacks the open relationality of the triadic form (105–121; 376f).

Kristeva's originality in analyzing Christianity hinges on her interpreting the loving God of the New Testament as a symbolic representative of the archaic, imaginary father. God represents not essentially the phallic father as law, as negation, as patriarchy, but the originary, pregenital third party, modeling and reflecting identity as love, affirmation, acceptance (47). In this image the Christian God marks the clearing of a space for triadic subjectivity (147). Not only is the symbolic realm of law and negation transmuted when it carries the image of this loving Original, it also tells the mythic drama of the son whose body is sacrificed and destroyed to overcome the negativity of the law, whose suffering and death make suffering and death themselves markers of the love that makes subject-being possible — culminating in the resurrection of the body (141 – 145). This affirmation and validation of subject-being, this fusion of semiotic and symbolic identity, is founded in the mythic Third Party, and it imagines and discursively sustains a triadic subject-space open to love, to another, to others and relationships, and the possibility of love of neighbor and even of enemy (146).

This symbolic, public mythologizing of the structures of the narcissan project supports a strong degree of sublimation. By figuring the third party as loving other and thus supporting the triadic openness of the self, this myth enables an essentially imaginary subjectivity to maintain a high degree of symbolic and social functionality. Yet there are also other factors at work, and dysfunctional dimensions of this strategy, as well as dysfunctional distortions of it, come into play. Kristeva does not focus on these in *Tales of Love*, but this discussion would be incomplete without them.

For example, the patriarchal structure of Christian communities tends to transform the imaginary father of the original myth into a phallic father who validates male identities while abjecting female ones. This destabilizes the triadic structure, reactivating the original terror and rage in the form of abjection of mother, for which the feminine in general becomes the symbolic and transferential representative and victim (PH 110–132).[2] On the other hand, to some extent at least, the figure of the Virgin offers a female and maternal image of identity ("Stabat Mater," passim; *In the Beginning* 42; *Tales of Love* 342). Totally emptied, viable precisely as the vessel of the paternal word, this figure incorporates abjection into its design of sublimation; yet even with its negativity, it has provided for many a significant stabilization of psychic space within a traditional Christian context. To the extent that the myth holds together the symbolic representation of the imaginary father as loving lawgiver and the symbolic representation of archaic mother as virgin mother, it sustains the triadic foundation of relational subjectivity, though at significant and unequal cost.

In the Middle Ages, St. Bernard uses the New Testamental relationality as background for his distinctive representation of self as essentially amorous passion directed to God as Loving Beloved (*Tales of Love* 161–167). In Thomas Aquinas, this Bernardine loving self is fused with elements of the Plotinian narcissism. Thomas takes over the whole relational symbolism of the Biblical myth, but in combining it with classical themes he makes a crucial shift. According to Thomas, the foundation of any love is necessarily self-love: we are permitted and called to love ourselves as the foundation of personal and ethical life. Subjective life is thus made viable by the Father's authorization of self-love (172–174).

Now, this love is inseparable from knowledge: I love what I know, and I love knowing, and I love by knowing (178 – 183). The rhetoric of originary love from the imaginary Third is bound to the rhetoric of self-reflection and self-contemplation, and the Bernardine subjectivity of passion is construed also as a Plotinian subject of contemplation. This opens the way to a reconfiguring of the loved/loving subjectivity of the New Testament and of Bernard on the basis of a knowing, self-loving subjectivity, a prototype of the *cogito, ergo sum* of Descartes (186, 378). This again, in the sequel if not in Thomas himself, collapses the ternary structure of the New Testament self into a binary one.

With the coming of modernity, this weakening of the openness of self to otherness is transmuted into a narcissistic intolerance of otherness: knowledge as self-loving contemplation goes over into knowledge as subjugation of otherness and difference: Galileo, for the physical world, and Sade, for the world of the erotic, express, she says, this same narcissistic annihilation of psychic space (378). I suggest that the third party is still present in modern subjectivity, but in an attenuated form as *world*, as nature, as object (abject?). The narcissistic rage then plays itself out as domination of the depersonalized other. The cognitive dynamics of this development, in the absence of a sustaining discourse of triadic identity, have led to the death of God, the final breakdown of this whole strategy for the symbolic structuration of psychic space. In the absence of adequate alternatives, the cover over original nothingness fails, and panic and rage and quasi-psychotic forms of personal identity become cultural stereotypes (373 – 375).

In the world that has resulted, does psychoanalysis take the place of religion? This is a central theme of Kristeva's little book, *In the Beginning Was Love: Psychoanalysis and Faith*. Psychoanalysis provides a discourse of love and desire, within which the previously inarticulable imaginings and desires of suffering individuals come to speech (IB 1 – 9). In discourse with an other, these imaginings and desires acquire that symbolic representability and relativity which free us to love and work and imagine and enjoy. The transference in which psychoanalytic discourse is founded is a quest for love, for the possibility that identity, desire, and the third party can coexist (3). In this contemporary situation, says Kristeva, faith (like the transference) is a strategy of self-relinquishment in order to receive beatitude; it, too, is a quest for love and for a discourse of coexistence (23 – 27). Christian faith, because of its rigidity and limited range of symbolic options, and its suppression of the erotic and imaginary character of its discourse, is not comparable to the outcome of analysis. But it is a transferential quest for love, and as such it is comparable to the entry into analysis (52).

The contents of faith are, as Freud observed, wishful. Kristeva enumerates some of those wishes: "The almighty father? Patients miss one, want one, or suffer from one" (40). "The representation of Christ's Passion signifies a guilt that is visited upon the son, who is himself put to death" (40). "A virgin mother? We want our mothers to be virgins, so that we can love them better, or allow ourselves to be loved by them without fear of a rival" (42). "More than one mother has been sustained in narcissistic equilibrium by the fantasy of having a child without the aid of a father" (42). She contrasts the idealizing character of these expressions to the specificity of analysis: "By shifting attention from the 'macrofantasy' to the 'microfantasy,' analysis reveals the underlying sexuality . . . ; for though the object of desire be transformed, desire itself remains a feature of Christian discourse" (44).

Adherents of this fantasy faith, Kristeva says,

> have already begun the analytic process. Is it not true that analysis begins with something comparable to faith, namely, transferential love? 'I trust you, and I expect something in return.' Analysis ends, however, with the realization that I cannot expect anything in return unless I am willing to give myself to my benefactor, that demands and desires make the subject the slave of its object. Once analyzed, I continue to make demands and to feel desires, but in full awareness of cause and effect. Knowledge of my desires is at once my freedom and my safety net. Now I can love and delude myself at my own risk. In this sense analysis is not less than religion but more — more, especially, than Christianity, which hews so closely to its fundamental fantasies. (52)

The superiority of analysis is thus not in the abolition of the imaginary, of the narcissistic, of desire and illusion. It is rather in their unmasking, the exposure of the personal and impersonal dynamics of their forms and effects. I do not bring all the unconscious to consciousness; I do not live without fantasy and desire and inner division. But I do acknowledge the other within, and the emptiness at the core of my subjectivity, and the fact that all my conscious activity, all my discourse, all my sense of self, is marked by this inner other and this emptiness. I may, indeed, love with all the narcissistic identification and illusory desire that constitutes that madness; yet when it crashes, I am not destroyed; even my surprise is partly the chagrined recognition that I have done it again. And I have entered into my illusion acknowledging all this, and at my own risk. (59–63)

What, then, of truth? If analysis is never truly completed, if illusion and desire continue to play a role in each life, including the life of the analyst, if unconscious desire always also speaks in the symbolic, even in psychoanalytic discourse itself, if the analyzed individual still lives with fictions, with constructs that always bear the semiotics of the unconscious, then the difference between psychoanalysis and faith can no longer be simply figured as "truth" vs. "illusion." Freud could confidently tell us, "Science is no illusion, but it would be an illusion to seek anywhere else what it can not give us" (*Future of an Illusion* 93). But in Kristeva's account, is there not necessarily an illusory, fictive dimension, an unconscious semiotics, to psychoanalysis itself? What is the relation between this illusion and the illusion of faith?

Kristeva indicates that the fictive play of the end of analysis differs from that of Christian faith in that its forms are optional, plural, variable; that its fictive character is explicit (at least intermittently and in principle); and that its erotic agenda is overt. Yet Christianity has long provided a public, interpersonal semiotic of identity and desire that has sustained and continues to sustain many lives. If the cure, too, is only a partial achievement, if post-cure illusions are to be assessed primarily by the balance between empowering and disempowering achieved in their symbolic mobilization of the semiotics of the imaginary, does the religious illusion then continue to offer options for human being?

That depends. It depends, it seems to me, on how the discourse of desire, of identity, of emptiness plays out across and with and through the discourse of God and Jesus and the church. It depends on whether the ancient battles of orthodoxy against heresy can be reinscribed as a defense of triadic openness against narcissistic alternatives. It depends on whether acknowledgment of the fictive and erotic dynamics of faith renews or dissolves the power of this semiotic to sustain not just individual lives but communities of moral and social practice.

It depends, too, on what the alternatives are. If the only alternatives are narcissistic symbolic systems founded either on mystic fusion or on a will to domination, or else abjective icons of terror and rage, nihilistic, addictive, and violent, it is premature to dismantle a historic and social semiotics that is rooted in the inseparability of personal identity from the acknowledgment of the third party, and that is still tacitly ingrained in the basic textures of our secular discourses of identity and coexistence and value.

Is there, then, a future for an imaginary, erotic, open, optional Christianity? This can only be matter for ongoing conversation and exploration in which nothing is guaranteed and nothing is ruled out. And in which we participate at our own risk.

## NOTES

1. Kristeva at times specifically speaks of the triadic structure itself as "narcissism" or "narcissistic" (e.g., 44, 374); sometimes she calls this "primary narcissism." At other times she seems to follow a more conventional usage in applying the word to the dyadic reduction (e.g., 109). I have inclined to the latter practice for the sake of clarity.

2. See also Martha Reineke, " 'The Devils Are Come Down Upon Us': Myth, History, and the Witch as Scapegoat" (*Union Seminary Quarterly Review,* Spring, 1990) and " 'This Is My Body': Reflections on Abjection, Anorexia, and Medieval Women Mystics" (*Journal of the American Academy of Religion,* LVIII, 2, Summer, 1990, 245–265).

## $\left(\text{INTER-TEXT } 3\right)$

I will not attempt to sustain the pretext of a critical discussion of my own essay. Instead, I will proceed directly to the issues raised by its conjunction with the others. The essay centers on Kristeva's account of the sublimatory functions of Christianity in sustaining personal viability and sociality, and on the transferential structure of faith as desire for love and thus as openness to change. Kearns, too, wishes to consider whether space is open for a religious life, indeed, for prayer, beyond the dissolvent import of a psychoanalytic critique as searching as that of Kristeva. She gives focal attention to the ambiguity of the figure of the father as the archaic model for subjectivity (see also Reineke) and as the phallic patriarch; recognizing the importance of the model, she also recognizes the need for any postmodern religiosity to get beyond the patriarch. Her notion of *prière féminine* seems to me just the sort of fictive religious practice I speak of at the end.

The most important issues I see between this essay and the others lie in its relation to Martha Reineke's. Here, as in other contexts where we compare our work, I find two key differences of emphasis, which seem to be systematically related to one another. Reineke centers appropriately on issues of gender, while I do not. The case for the viability of existence in Christian terms is easier to make in an essay that does not focus on those specific issues. Reineke also attends especially to those aspects of Christianity, and of Kristeva's analyses of it, that show it as violent, negative, dysfunctional, especially for women. This essay, on the other hand, pursues a hermeneutics of recovery, attempting to discern what worked, what might be retrievable from the site after the metaphysical and absolutist structures have been dismantled and hauled away.

I do not believe there is any fundamental conflict between these two approaches — though a reader must beware of the man (editor, even) who minimizes the difference in the woman's voice. I believe Reineke is right, and it is important to track, that Christianity achieves its forms of viability at a cost, and a cost that falls heavily on the bodies of women. If any elements of Christian imagery, of the Christian econ-

65

omy of self and love and sin and forgiveness in which the name of God circulates, can contribute to the fictive practices we need for postmodern and post-Christian existence, they must be scrutinized by a rigorous hermeneutics of suspicion, in which their support for patriarchy is unmasked, ironised, disarmed.

At the same time I believe that Kristeva is right to find in the Christian figures of self and love affirmative strategies of existence and co-existence and not merely pathologies. The modern unmasking of our illusions has brought the present age into the neighborhood of a nihilism that externalizes our core nothingness in the form of a devaluation and destruction of everything else, to such an extent that I think it urgent to retrieve, deconstructed and ironised, whatever part-images, transitional images, compromises, fantasies may be available in the tradition. In pursuing such images, aided by Kristeva, we see an ironic side to Gadamer's idea of effective history, the history of the working out of the effects of a text: the terms in which we are constituted and by which we articulate our post-Christian autonomy are themselves consequences, residues, of the history of those very Christian illusions we wish to move beyond.

The other overall difference between our approaches is that I settle for attention to the texts and to the existential dynamics of embodied subjectivity as articulated by and against those texts. Reineke seeks a more direct engagement with social practices, the public structurings of embodiment in which societies, and specific inscriptions of gender, are constituted and enacted. It is partly for this reason that she brings Kristeva together with Rene Girard, whose approach is less literary and more anthropological and social. Again, I do not see a central disagreement here so much as a different style, a different personal path and social location.

I do not suppose at all that Reineke disagrees with me here. I intend only to articulate the particular grounds for my adopting a more recovery-oriented hermeneutic orientation. If there is a substantive disagreement between us, it may lie in the relation between the images of the archaic mother and the father of individual prehistory, on the one hand, and the issue of the feminine, of woman, of her identity, on the other. I believe that the archaic figures are in Kristeva's account prior to gender difference and that they have the same sorts of semiotic and narcissistic function in personal identity for all of us, subject to subsequent discursive constructions. I think this relativizes the question of gender in a radical way. I am not clear whether Reineke does or does not agree with this.

# 4

# THE MOTHER IN MIMESIS:
## Kristeva and Girard on Violence and the Sacred

### Martha Reineke

*Martha Reineke's essay begins in a space marked out by Freud's* Totem and Taboo *with its myth of the primal murder by which society is founded, and explores some ways in which René Girard's specific elaboration of this problematic is illuminated and corrected by Kristeva's theory of narcissism in* Tales of Love *and of abjection in* Powers of Horror. *Reineke's reading relocates the victim of the primal murder from the father to the mother.*

In an essay, "Women, the sacred and money," Luce Irigaray raises some provocative questions about the religious dimension of human life. Noting the prevalence of sacrifice within religious traditions, Irigaray states that most societies are founded on sacrifice: sacrifice is "an immolation that brings the social space into being."[1] Irigaray concurs with René Girard, who also recognizes the centrality of sacrifice to the formation of human society. Yet she criticizes him for offering a gender-neutral theory of sacrifice. Noting that, apart from a cursory discussion of Dionysus' female companions, Girard does not explore the place of women in sacrificial traditions, Irigaray poses a series of questions intended to highlight the significance of gender to any theory of sacrifice and societal formation.

Irigaray's queries focus on two substitutions that characterize sacrificial traditions. She suggests that attention to these substitutions will enable her to outline a gendered theory of sacrifice. Alluding to Girard's theory, Irigaray considers an initial exchange: a sacrificial victim always lies hidden from view beneath the body of another victim who is visible. She wonders about the subjective and objective conditions under which this substitution of victims is staged.

Examining a second substitution, Irigaray muses about the exchange of words for rite:

> Why did speech fail? What was missing? Why kill, cut up and eat
> as a sign of covenant? To abolish some sort of violence? What sort?
> Where does it originate? And isn't it possible to analyze why
> speech was so inadequate that such an act became necessary? Was
> it, for instance, because of a lack of harmony between words, acts
> and bodies?[2]

Highlighted by Irigaray's comments about language and violent
acts is a somatic hinge: the human body from which both violent words
and acts issue.

According to Irigaray, the substitutions she cites — body for body,
rite for words — found the sacrificial economy. Moreover, she suggests
that, however well disguised, considerations of gender are paramount
in these exchanges. In respect to both the choice of victims and the form
of rites, women are subject to a form of sociality in which they "remain
an inert body, paralysed in and through cultural bonds which aren't
their own."[3]

Regrettably, having posed these questions, Irigaray does not go on
to offer sustained commentary on them. Instead, Irigaray's inquiry
serves as a vehicle by means of which she can gain distance from the
sacrificial economy to explore the terrain of an alternative economy less
hostile to women.

Staying with Irigaray's provocative questions where she has not,
in this essay I address questions of gender that arise from an examination of a social space determined by sacrifice. I turn, as did Irigaray, to
the work of René Girard to explore with him the contours of violence. I
extend Irigaray's criticisms of Girard even as I retrieve from Girard aspects of his theory that support a gender-sensitive theory of sacrifice
and societal formation.

Significant to my project is the relation Girard forges between religion, violence, and language. Girard locates the roots of violence in a
murder traceable, as it were, to the origins of human culture. The structure of language conceals this murder; myth and ritual represent it
when they reenact the sacrificial resolution of the mimetic crisis that
fueled the violence.

Wanting to elaborate on Girard's thesis in gender-sensitive ways,
I place his theory under the lens of Julia Kristeva's feminist hermeneutic. I argue that this lens reveals violence directed against the figure of

the mother, which is sustained by the linguistic code of patriarchy and manifested in its religion. With the ontological heart of the problem of violence in patriarchal culture thus exposed, Kristeva's and Girard's theses are joined. The one who Girard has said is barred from language, whose murder language conceals and ritual represents, is the mother whom Kristeva has said patriarchy denies: our linguistic and cultural codes are structured around the murder of the mother.

My efforts to reflect on Irigaray's questions advance as a result of the linkage of Kristeva and Girard that I espouse. The murdered figure over whose body society and language have arisen is hidden no longer by a pattern of substitution that conceals her identity. Further, that Kristeva reveals the first victim of sacrifice as female supports a gender-sensitive analysis of the failure of speech and the onset of violent acts, for which ritual sacrifice substitutes.

## I. GIRARD: MIMESIS AND MURDER

In *Violence and the Sacred*,[4] Girard places violence at the origins of human language and culture. All language and institutions are structured by that event, and rituals do but represent or reenact it. These linguistic and cultural structures do not expressly name the originative event; rather, we learn of that event indirectly when we note that language, institutions, and rituals seem to be shaped in a particular way and in service to a particular objective. They function to conceal something or someone. When we ask what or who is being concealed by the shaping, veiling function of language and culture, we uncover a murder. We arrive at the site of the originative murder when we attend to two mechanisms that found the linguistic code which shapes how we experience the world: the mechanism of mimetic desire and of the surrogate victim.

The mechanism of mimetic desire structures the human subject's acquisition of the world. Desire is shaped in imitation of an other, who is identified by Girard, not as the father of Freud's Oedipal theory, but in gender-neutral fashion as the model.[5] By contrast also to Freud, desire is not directed toward an object of the model's desire, as Freud thought, but is rooted simply in the quest to be like the other. Desiring what the other desires because of the prior, and more basic, desire to be like the other, the human subject notes that the closer he or she comes to acquisition of the object of the model's desire and, through that acquisition, to the model, the greater is the rejection or refusal of the subject by the model.[6] Veneration and rejection, mimesis and difference structure the subject's experience of the world, until, in a shocking denouement of the dynamics of rivalry that sees the difference between the subject and its model obliterated by their common desire, the model becomes the monstrous double by whom the subject is repulsed and from whom she or he seeks distance.[7] Desire has become death.

This mimetic crisis is writ large in culture. Memories common to each human are erased in the successful displacement of aggression and guilt onto a sacrificial victim. A mimetic free-for-all gives way to polarization on a particular target: the scapegoat.[8] The scapegoat as mimetic substitute is a monstrous double to be condemned. But in death, the scapegoat is an object of veneration.[9] Taking the community's violence with him or her, the scapegoat enables the community to return to stasis.

The conclusion of the sacrificial crisis announces a resolution in the subject's quest for being. The subject had sought in the model the being it lacked. In the violent culmination of its sacred quest, an object of sacrifice confers that plenitude of being.[10] Subsequently, myth and ritual become "the first fruits of an endeavor to think this miracle of a collective murder that restores peace."[11] Indeed, they perpetuate and renew it.

Conceived in terms of language, we can say that a linguistic phylogeny recapitulates a linguistic ontogeny. The mechanism of the surrogate victim gives birth to language: it is the first object of language. Establishing difference where once there were only doubles and stability of meaning where once there was only violent reciprocity, language is a divine epiphany. Violence becomes the signifier of being, the signifier of divinity.[12]

Two aspects of Girard's theory link it in significant ways with Kristeva's. First, Girard roots the process of mimetic desire in a pre-Oedipal drama. Citing Freud's comments on identification and noting that Freud set these comments aside in his consideration of the Oedipal complex, Girard returns to the site of primary identification to retrace its contours. Remarking that the model directs the disciple's desire to a particular object by desiring it himself, Girard notes that mimetic desire is rooted neither in the subject, who in familial language is the child, nor in the object-mother, but in a third party whose desire is imitated by the subject.[13] The child seeks to appropriate the model to itself by taking over the things that belong to the father-model. This identification prepares the way for the Oedipus complex, but the direction of desire is different. Identification, not desire for an object-mother, comes first. Criticizing the philosophy of consciousness that led Freud to underplay the significance of the *mimetic triangle* and focus his attention on the Oedipal drama, Girard argues that only careful attention to the former can account for humans' entry into language and culture and for the violence that accompanies that entry.[14] Indeed, without that attention to the turbulent dynamics of identification, violence is mystified. Attributed to the death drive, instinct, or impulse, violence is then removed from human culture and the arena of human responsibility.

Girard's effort to come to grips with violence by placing it at the roots of human life and society is evident also in another aspect of his theory of which we hear echoes in Kristeva's work. Girard turns to Freud's *Totem and Taboo* to locate there the patterns of the mimetic and sacrificial crises he has traced previously in a familial drama. According to Girard, Freud's insights never have been appreciated fully. A theoretical formulation that would link sacrificial practices—in all their richness and detail—to actual incidents of violence eluded Freud. Able to forge ties between sacrificial rites and societal conflict only at one point in time— a single act of murder committed in prehistory—Freud sought more stable ground and located the dynamics of patricide and the incest prohibition in the psyche rather than in history.

Returning to the path that Freud abandoned, Girard notes the tension—unresolved in *Totem and Taboo*—between violent deeds and complexes. Freud, unable to place patricide securely at the origins of history, relinquished his claim on the social roots of violence with one hand, only to reinstate that claim with the other. When Freud acknowledged that the prohibition on incest not only corresponds to a repressed desire of the Oedipus complex, but also has "a powerful practical basis,"[15] he returned to the social context. If the dead father resides only in wishes of those under the sway of the Oedipus complex, the prohibition of incest yet proscribes real deeds.

Because the brothers in the primitive horde who banded together to overcome the father were rivals of each other in regard to women, only a law against incest could make human society possible. That the brothers, in Freud's account, ultimately prepare to engage each other as if the father never existed suggests to Girard the most compelling insight of *Totem and Taboo*. When the threat of violence shifts to the brothers—each the other's rival and each indistinguishable from the other— a drama once confined to the familial stage moves into a larger arena.[16] Read in terms of mimetic and sacrificial crises, the themes of *Totem and Taboo* take root in society: the incest taboo, writ large, signals society's birth.

That the father as the signifier of violence explains nothing is, according to Girard, Freud's most significant insight in *Totem and Taboo*. Human community is brought into existence only as mimetic struggles of its members with each other are neutralized by a violence inflicted on a surrogate victim.[17] Maintaining in his own theory only the structure of reciprocal violence highlighted by Freud, Girard sees mimetic and sacrificial crises played out repeatedly in culture. For Girard, these patterns of crisis and not the familial themes of patricide and the incest prohibition survive *Totem and Taboo* as its major insight.

Precisely because he believes that familial language is irrelevant to the key argument of *Totem and Taboo*, the structure of sacrifice uncovered in *Totem and Taboo* serves Girard as a paradigm of societal creation: all cultures are founded on the murder of a surrogate victim. Moreover, because the prohibition against incest marks the origin of all cultural interdictions, *Totem and Taboo* is paradigmatic for the religious dimension of human life as well. The contexts of prohibitions may differ — food, weapons, land, women — but their sacrificial structure remains the same. Prohibitions enable a community to set itself off forever from the maelstrom of reciprocal violence — the dizzying confrontation with the monstrous double — that has snared it. The religious rituals that mark these prohibitions enable each society to both commemorate the crisis that signaled its beginnings and manage further confrontations in ways that do not put an entire community at risk. Religion "humanizes violence"[18] by purging from human memory the actual conditions under which human society arose and is maintained. Empowering a community to acknowledge the forces that elicit violent acts, religion also grants distance: the participants in ritual are but passive agents of powers that lie beyond them.[19]

## II. KRISTEVA: MIMESIS, MOTHER, AND MURDER

Kristeva shares much in common with Girard. Like Girard, she roots human entry into language and society — in its fragility and propensity for violence — in a pre-Oedipal drama. Also like Girard, Kristeva turns to *Totem and Taboo* in her efforts to understand language, violence, and the sacred. At the same time, Kristeva differs in significant ways from Girard. With Kristeva as my guide, I now retrace steps previously taken with Girard and uncover, as Girard has not, the central figure of the mother.

A Kristeva-inspired reading of Girard advances my efforts to re-spond to Irigaray's provocative questions. Kristeva accounts for the con-cealment of the mother behind sacrificial substitutes in rituals that, rep-licating our murderous origins, enable us to manage the legacy of violence deeded to us by our birth. Moreover, in tracing the subjective and objective conditions of substitution, Kristeva sheds light on Irigar-ay's primary concerns: she accounts for the failure of speech to stem the violence that accompanies societal formation or reformation, and she of-fers insights concerning the prominence of alimentary motifs in the vio-lence stemming from that failure.

Kristeva locates the birth of the human subject in primary narcis-sism. As Girard has argued also, Kristeva states that the narcissistic structure which first positions the subject in the world is a triad. Held in place by twin magnets of attraction—a father of individual prehistory and an archaic mother — a fragile and unstable subject hangs sus-pended between them.[20] Who are these parents whose relation to the subject predates the Oedipal drama?

Kristeva places them in a ternary structure that in its first stage re-veals itself in "mimetic play" over emptiness. Viewed both in terms of the Saussurian sign that places one in front of a bar and in terms of La-can's gaping hole, this narcissistic play screens emptiness, or lines it.[21] Thus, for Kristeva the twin parties to narcissism both protect empti-ness, causing it to exist, and guarantee that their child can bridge emp-tiness to enter language and society.

Like Girard, Kristeva describes this process in terms of primary identification focused on a pre-Oedipal father. In language remarkably similar to Girard's, she argues that mimeticism is nonobjectal. She writes that one identifies "not with an object, but with what offers itself to me as a model."[22] Efforts to incorporate the model, to assume its being as one's own, recall processes of oral maternal assimilation but are distinct from it. Because the pre-object to be incorporated is given in language, when the child assimilates the paternal model to itself it swallows words. In reproducing the other's words, having and being merge for the child: it becomes like the other.

Although Kristeva attributes primary identification to a father, be-cause the mimetic process predates the Oedipal stage and sexual differ-ence, the twin poles of the mimetic process pertain not so much to pa-rental roles understood empirically as to the structure of being interpreted ontologically. To study primary narcissism as a triadic struc-ture is to return to borderline states—the imaginary, in Lacanian terms

— in order to explore the birth of a subject in language. Reference is made to paternal *and* maternal modes because they enable one to hold to a ridge between connection and distance, fulfillment and emptiness, in order to follow that process of displacement through which an embodied being becomes an expressive organism and finds itself constituted in the very opposition between presence and absence.[23]

Distinguished from the metonymic object of desire — Lacan's *petit autre* — the object of identification that Kristeva cites is metaphoric.[24] Kristeva's notion of metaphoricity counters Lacan, who has said that the human, in its education to the symbolic, necessarily is set adrift never to be the all for another that promises unity and being. In distinction from Lacan, who tells his story for that sadder but wiser adult, Kristeva uncovers a playful tale of promise at the zero degree of subjectivity.[25] In this love story, at the very splitting that establishes the psyche, the subject uncovers an open space and is supported in being between the One and an Other. Because love promises that for the One there is an Other, love promises being in difference. In theological terms, it promises God.

Experienced only indirectly, as a logical possibility of language, the metaphoricity of being is testified to by sounds "on the fringe of my being that transfer me to the place of the Other."[26] Apparent not in the words of the symbolic that would seek to master space, but only in the sonorous quality of those words, this metaphoricity anchors one in being.

Nevertheless, if such anchoring always already secures the subject in being, we err if we forget that the "narcissistic parry" reaches out over an abyss.[27] Like Girard, Kristeva understands that primary identification is fraught with danger. Precisely because the parental poles are held in place only because of the maternal desire for the phallus, the subject's quest for being is a painful one: the other does not want me, but another. The subject necessarily confronts the radical emptiness of being.[28]

Moreover, like Girard, Kristeva perceives violence in the quest for being. Girard, as we recall, positions violence in the escalation of the mimetic struggle between model and disciple, in which the cancellation of difference between them leads the disciple to desperate measures in an effort to recover difference when challenged by a monstrous and threatening double. Interestingly, it appears that for Girard, under the conditions of crisis, the original triadic structure of mimesis becomes a dyad. The object of desire fades from the view of the disciple and model who, mirroring an escalating violence for each other, are caught in a double bind — each a lethal threat to the other — until their violence can be visited on a scapegoat-sacrifice through whom difference can be reinstated.

By contrast to Girard, Kristeva maintains the triadic form of primary identification in her analysis, which we can attribute in part to her continued reliance on familial language. The mother-object does not fade from view in the crisis of primary narcissism. Violence haunts a ternary structure of narcissism when access to psychic space promised by the imaginary eludes the child. Kristeva writes of this violence: "I imagine a child who has swallowed up his parents too soon . . . and to save himself, rejects and throws up everything that is given to him. . . . Even before things for him are . . . he drives them out . . . and constitutes his own territory, edged by the abject. . . . What he has swallowed up instead of maternal love is an emptiness, or rather a maternal hatred without a word for the words of the father; that is what he tries to cleanse himself of, tirelessly."[29]

The child in exile from the psychic space promised by the imaginary strays and does not get its bearings. Asking, "where am I?" instead of "who am I?," the child who experiences abjection is no longer supported in being by the parental poles of possibility that bridge emptiness. Foundering, this child risks at every moment a fall into the abyss. Given that threat, the child seeks to maintain itself in the Other through a sacrificial strategy not dissimilar from that employed by the twin protagonists of Girard's mimetic drama. Having been led astray on the path to embodied expression, the child now explores the dark side of being and seeks to incorporate a devouring mother in order to give birth to itself in that way. Falling back on the archaic possibilities of oral assimilation—now perceived in terms of reciprocal threat—the child will bite before being bitten.[30]

In contrast to the child for whom the imaginary has constituted a successful bridge to the symbolic, the subject of abjection is beset by ambiguities. The imagery of abjection may be inscribed symbolically, but the terror so inscribed recalls a prior moment marking always the margins, borders, and refuse of being where outside and inside merge and can annihilate the one who would climb free of the abyss. Without the ladder to the symbolic offered to the child by the imaginary father, the mother is the primary site of abjection. Fluids from her body evoke for the child its violent expulsion from the maternal interior in all of its risk. Her blood and milk — source of life and death, nourishment and threat—are first witness to the drama of archaic differentiation.[31]

Like Girard, Kristeva appeals to *Totem and Taboo* when she claims that violence transpires precisely in the absence of the father of individual prehistory. Reflecting on the two taboos of totemism — murder and incest—Kristeva notes a slippage in the Freudian argument. Freud virtually sets aside the origins of incest dread to attend to murder, that keystone of the Oedipal structure. Kristeva, like Girard, aims to give incest its due, for she also sees that reflection on incest is crucial to any theory that would analyze violence, societal formation, and religion.

In distinction from Girard, however, Kristeva maintains the significance of gender in the drama that engages the horde of brothers in violent struggle. Girard thinks that he can account for violence in society only if gender and the familial drama are irrelevant to the underlying pattern of violence that structures human community. By contrast, Kristeva reclaims the literal significance of the incest prohibition. Although she would concur with Girard that the incest prohibition is fundamental to societal formation, she would insist that, if a theory is to account adequately for the violence which accompanies the birth of human society and for the prohibitions meant to keep that violence in check, it must demonstrate attentiveness to the material reality of *embodied* prohibitions. Accordingly, that the brothers fight over the bodies of *women* is not incidental. For, if *Totem and Taboo* tells in mythological form of the birth of society, the confrontation with the feminine registered there is, above all, a confrontation with the abject mother.

Kristeva's discovery of both the centrality of the figure of the mother for societal formation and the role of violence within that process is based on her reading of a bipolar sacred in *Totem and Taboo*. Whereas the aspect of the sacred most familiar to a reader of Freud is that associated with the sacrificial exchange of the father for a totem animal, Kristeva reminds us that *Totem and Taboo* begins with an evocation of taboo: the dread of incest. Claiming that its pages are "haunted" by the mother-image, Kristeva argues that *Totem and Taboo* speaks of another sacred "oriented toward those uncertain spaces of unstable identity, toward the fragility — both threatening and fusional — of the archaic dyad."[32]

Exploring this facet of the sacred, which Kristeva identifies as the "true lining of the sacrificial,"[33] Kristeva determines that it is structured by spatial ambivalence. An ambiguity of perception—a confusion of inside and outside, pleasure and pain—attends the psychosomatic reality of this other side of the sacred. Tracing the contours of uncertainty, Kristeva claims that this aspect of the sacred is assigned the task of warding off the danger posed by the mother. Rituals of interdiction mark the threat to the subject — that he or she may sink irretrievably into the mother— *and* structure a protective space. Rituals establish the boundaries, however archaic, of the human subject's proper self. The incest

*5ee Doyle*

prohibition, a paradigm of all such interdictory processes, functions to throw a veil over primary narcissism, a veil that blocks forever the menace to identity found there: the fluctuation of inside/outside, pleasure/pain, word/deed.[34]

Probing the mother's role in the interdictory processes that inscribe boundaries, Kristeva borrows language from anthropologist Mary Douglas. From Douglas, she takes the notion of "the excluded" as the basis for religious prohibition. Kristeva notes that, in a number of societies, religious rites function to separate groups differentiated by class, gender, or age *by means of prohibiting a filthy, defiling element*. A rite of purification serves as a "ridge" separating that which is abominated (the abject) from that which is whole and clean. Indeed, defilement *is* that which has been jettisoned from the social system, for order (that which is clean) is inscribed on the social aggregate only as disorder (dirt) is proscribed.[35]

Extending Douglas's insights, Kristeva establishes the logic of abjection and documents its maternal cast. Although abjection may be variously coded — defilement, food taboo, sin — it follows a common pattern. In its most basic form — defilement — the logic of abjection enables the human subject to come into being as an expressive organism. Neither sign nor matter, defilement is a translinguistic spoor of the most archaic boundaries of one's clean and proper body.[36] Belonging to "a scription without signs,"[37] defilement constitutes the most basic mapping of meaning at the somatic hinge of human being.

If Kristeva has shared with Girard an analysis of the logic of interdiction, her reflections on "defilement" distance Kristeva from Girard and advance our understanding of the domestication of sacrifice in acts of ritual prohibition. "Defilement" functions as Kristeva's Rosetta stone, enabling her to read the linguistic code of patriarchy as Girard has not. She can demonstrate that our linguistic and cultural codes are structured around the murder of the mother because defilement accounts for the myriad substitutions that have functioned to conceal the gender of the victim over whose body society has arisen.

The opposition between the pure and impure is "a coding of the differentiation of the speaking subject as such."[38] Prior to or more basic than the coding of difference by the symbolic, purity and impurity mark the subject's repulsion from the (m)other. Although the oppositional structure of defilement mimics the violent logic of the symbolic — sacrificer/sacrifice/God; subject/thing/meaning[39] — the object of violence is displaced or denied in defilement. Not bound by a signifying dimension, rituals of purification demarcate materially, actively, translinguistically.[40] A binary logic of borders is impressed on the human subject by its mother before the human subject accedes to the father's law: her blood speaks to the subject of life and death; sphincteral training evokes for the subject a struggle with mother for a clean and proper self.

In a parceling of the human body, pollution is rendered schematically. Excrement and its equivalents (decay, infection, disease) stand for the danger to identity from without; menstrual and birthing blood represent the danger from within.[41] Both form the pretext for ritual and myth as phylogeny recapitulates ontogeny: the former bounding society against threats from without; the latter protecting society from dangers issuing from within.

This semiotic rendering of the body (individual and social) is a precondition of language itself. Language represses this corporeal mapping of maternal authority, but the incest prohibition assigned to monitor repression is weak. Neither the abject nor the demoniacal potential of the feminine are banned sufficiently. Speaking being still attempts to express in ritual his or her advent into an ever fragile, ever threatened order. Often, alimentary motifs — material witnesses to that archaic struggle with the mother — predominate. Kristeva traces a typology of catastrophe that is the abject through paganism, Judaism, and Christianity.

Paganism wards off the mother through elaborate rituals that separate the pure from the impure. Whether the impure be food or fire touched by a woman's hands or her blood, always, in its generative power, it is potentially deadly. The fire that cooks food does not necessarily purify it; in fact, fire may pollute food—necessitating ritual cleansing. Because fire and food point to the boundary between society and nature, which the act of cooking violates, cooked foods function as oral abjects, marking also the ambiguous boundary between the human and its first other: mother. Similarly, food remainders threaten. In their incompleteness, they are "residues of something, but especially of someone."[42]

Judaism cuts off the mother. Judaism inscribes impurity in an abstract moral register as potential for abomination, but not before it pays its last debt to nature. The rite of circumcision carves definitive protection against pollution onto every male body. In repetition of the knife that cuts the umbilical cord, the knife that cuts the flesh of the foreskin "displaces through ritual the preeminent separation, which is that from the mother."[43] That pains are taken in Leviticus to condemn all other cuttings and marks on the human body (Leviticus 19:27–28) as abominations before God underscores the point: the ambiguity of human corporeality is countered by an act that offers decisive protection against maternal impurity. All traces of the maternal body are lost to a new identity. Circumcision bonds speaking being to God.

Judaism moves away from the material register and its attendant sacrifices even as it radicalizes separation. Judaism thus "throttles murder": the female is a threat to be contained, not destroyed. The borders of symbolic order are transposed from the body to the temple. Food, death, and the female are dangerous, not because they are occasions for impurity, but because they are occasions for idolatry. Rejection of food or of the mother are mere pre-texts for a symbolic relation between Israel and God.[44] The pre-texts secure the existence of the One, but are without sacrality themselves. That circumcision separates Israelite men from the impurity of women is then significant only as a sign of alliance with Yahweh.

In its notion of sin, Christianity interiorizes Jewish abomination, absorbing abjection in speech through subjection to God of a speaking being who is divided within and who precisely through speech does not cease to purge himself or herself of impurities.[45] Evil, displaced into the subject, torments but not as polluting substance. Instead, evil is met as an "ineradicable repulsion of divided and contradictory being":[46] Christianity binges on and purges the mother. By that token, Christianity is a revenge of paganism, a "reconciliation with the maternal principle,"[47] except that the mother, swallowed up, is not for that matter revalorized or rehabilitated by Christianity. Of the nourishing and threatening heterogeneity of the maternal principle, Christianity keeps only the idea of sinning flesh.[48]

The division of Christian consciousness finds its catharsis in the Eucharist. Identifying abjection as a fantasy of devouring, Christianity effects its abreaction. "This is my body" mingles themes of devouring with those of satiating. Removing guilt from the archaic relation to the abject of need — the mother — the Eucharistic narrative "tames cannibalism."[49] The body of Christ, both body and spirit, nature and speech, promises reconciliation. Absorbed in the symbolic and no longer a being of abjection, the Christian is a lapsing subject.[50]

Even so, the account with the archaic mother is not yet settled. That what I call "bulimic Christianity" pays a price for interiorizing terror as self-error is visible most clearly in the late medieval women mystics. They live out the multivalent possibilities of the Eucharist—a food that we crave and that we consume—at the fount of infinite *jouissance*.[51] Exhibiting in large numbers the symptoms of self-starvation,[52] these women identify with Christ both as victims of abjection and as aggres-

sors in struggle against it. With their bodies they share the guilt of lapsing—the torment of the murderous subject. With their souls they share
in the sacrifice of self that lays anger to rest. Murdering and murdered,
they fight an archaic battle—in all its abjection—to the edge of death.

That their battles are overseen by confessors introduces a troubling new dynamic of abjection in Western culture. In confession one
disgorges sin in words. This is freedom, but it also delivers one over to
death because it permits conscription of the archaic by the Law of the
Father who, in the form of priestly authority, determines whether one's
words come from God or the devil.[53]

Kristeva believes that we are only now witnesses to the deadly
fruit of this new dynamic. In a secular society, discourse, no longer attended by a priest, lives out the fate of the abject under the auspices of
deregulated, deconstructed order. Faced with the whirl of abjection to
be written and to be spoken, those who have tracked the sacrificial economy to this point must consider whether this whirl portends carnival or
apocalypse.[54] Do we swallow words of death, or do we vomit up mother
death? Do words kill us or are they our freedom? Kristeva tells us that
the abject is still with us. The typology of catastrophe is still intact. We
dance today atop a volcano.

### III. CONCLUSION

Having begun this essay with Irigaray's questions about the religious
dimension of human life and the sacrificial economy that shapes it, I
conclude with Kristeva's observation that this violent economy remains
with us. Accompanied by Kristeva, I have followed Irigaray's questions
to conclusions that are both striking and unsettling. Having established
that Kristeva shares her basic thesis with Irigaray and Girard—our linguistic and cultural codes are structured by sacrifice — my further reflections on Kristeva have demonstrated that Kristeva's theory is distinguished from Irigaray and Girard's on two other counts, which prove
significant for a feminist analysis of the relation between violence,
women, and the sacred.

Where Irigaray has distanced herself from the sacrificial economy
to explore the terrain of an alternative economy less hostile to women,
Kristeva stays on to explore the sacrificial economy because, feminist
criticism notwithstanding, she believes that we continue to be shaped
by an economy of sacrifice even in a secular age. Where Girard, in his
evocation of religious practices that "domesticate" our violent origins,

has privileged those rituals that, replicating sacrificial substitution of a scapegoat, resolve the mimetic crisis, Kristeva attends to the dark side of the sacred, still shaped by crisis. For Kristeva, as I have indicated, the sacred is characterized not only by rituals that reinstate a social bond and restore authority after the death of the archaic father, but also by rituals oriented toward another drama: the birth of the subject in the imaginary.

In distinction from Girard, Kristeva explores how societies code themselves to accompany the subject on a journey of abjection. She suggests that, through aversion to incest, societies recall the uncertainties of primary narcissism where the child has risked, not a loss of part — castration by refusal of the Law — but its whole being.[55] Purification rites, food taboos, and pollution fears comprise a constellation of religious behaviors whose logic is governed by the threat to survival experienced in the ambiguities of primary narcissism when the most archaic and fragile boundaries of human subjectivity are first drawn.

Kristeva would argue that Girard's theory of a linguistic recapitulation of a founding event overlooks these other rituals because he has neglected the embodied, somatic aspects proper to the crises through which one is born into society: before the law bounds human society, the body bounds it. Thus, Kristeva would note a continued truth in Freud's theory of the death drive that Girard has rejected. Where Girard has thought that drive theory removes violence from the social stage where alone it is available for our consideration, Kristeva would emphasize that violence is writ large in society but it is not born there. Tracing its lineage to the pre-Oedipal drama, Kristeva would invite Girard to stay at the ridge between nature and culture to glimpse the subject at the moment of its bloody birth.

That Girard has overlooked key facets of the sacrificial economy may be attributed, I have suggested, to androcentric presuppositions, which have led him to disavow the relevance of gender to the incest prohibition and to retain only the notion of reciprocal violence when he discusses religion. Kristeva, by contrast, does develop a gender-sensitive theory of sacrifice and societal formation. Focusing her attention on the somatic hinge of being and tracing its contours, Kristeva detects there a pattern of substitution that hides the first victim of sacrifice: the mother. Moreover, in exploring the lack of harmony at that somatic hinge — visible in the alimentary motif of maternal violence — Kristeva notes the pervasiveness of the logic of abjection she has uncovered previously. Persisting in a secular age, this logic accounts for the shape of violent acts even today: when words fail, one bites to avoid being bitten.

What are the implications of Kristeva's conclusion for theology? Kristeva's study of abjection warns of dangers that still attend patriarchal religions, which have heretofore alternated between a vision of woman as angel and as whore, goddess of light and of darkness, guardian of order and bringer of chaos. Kristeva's work suggests that woman and her body cannot continue to bear alone the weight of the barred sacred. To try to do so is to bend the sacred to the point of breaking, the burden of which falls again on women: in accusations of witchcraft, bodily mutilations such as anorexia or clitoridectomy, woman battering, or woman-hating pornography. Rituals that diffuse the terror, that spread its weight around, are needed.

If paganism is not the best model, it is a model that, having dealt more honestly with the terrors of abjection than has Christianity, can offer one instructive insight: pollution rituals that counter the dangerous powers of the mother are found most often in those societies where the paternity of the father is most problematic.[56] Our own society has, in this respect, much in common with tribes such as the Bemba. Under the Law of the Father, we have a strange paternity: impregnation by the Word. On the one hand, the assignment of paternity to the symbolic order, in which woman does not exist, does offer comfort against the threat of abjection. But, on the other hand, because woman, on the borders of the Law, is assigned, alone in her maternity, not only the role of creator, in all its ecstasy, but also the role of destroyer and because that watchman, repression, is an unreliable sort, the Law of the Father is hazardous to woman's health.

For these reasons, Kristeva's constructive proposal in *Tales of Love* forms a suggestive counterpoint to *Powers of Horror.* To the extent that paternity could be located in the imaginary, with the pre-object mother and father of individual prehistory, women might achieve a respite from the terrors of history. If the sternness of the Father who brings about separation, judgment, and identity can be shaken, "far from leaving us orphaned or inexorably psychotic," such an unsettling action will reveal "multiple and varied destinies for paternity — notably of archaic, imaginary paternity."[57] Though one will still be unable to evade the Oedipal destiny that alone grants one entry into society, the promise of the imaginary may yet persist. Making possible one's entry also into a disposition that is playful and sublimational, the imaginary may then counter the tragic dynamic of a sacrificial economy with a promise of love as the "builder of spoken spaces."[58]

## NOTES

1. Luce Irigaray, "Women, the sacred and money," *Paragraph*, Vol. 8, 1986: 6.

2. Irigaray, 7.

3. Irigaray, 9.

4. René Girard, *Violence and the Sacred*, trans. Patrick Gregory (Baltimore: The Johns Hopkins University Press, 1977).

5. Girard, *Violence and the Sacred* 170.

6. Girard, *Violence and the Sacred* 146–47.

7. Girard, *Violence and the Sacred* 160–61.

8. René Girard, "Discussion," *Violent Origins: Walter Burkert, René Girard, and Jonathon Z. Smith on Ritual Killing and Cultural Formation*," ed. Robert G. Hamerton-Kelly (Stanford: Stanford University Press, 1987), 125–26.

9. Girard, *Violence and the Sacred* 86, 161.

10. Girard, *Violence and the Sacred* 146.

11. Girard, *Violence and the Sacred* 235.

12. Girard, *Violence and the Sacred* 131.

13. Girard, *Violence and the Sacred* 170.

14. Girard, *Violence and the Sacred* 176.

15. Girard, *Violence and the Sacred* 211.

16. Girard, *Violence and the Sacred* 212.

17. Girard, *Violence and the Sacred* 217–18.

18. Girard, *Violence and the Sacred* 134.

19. Girard, *Violence and the Sacred* 134.

20. Julia Kristeva, *Tales of Love*, trans. Leon S. Roudiez (New York: Columbia University Press, 1987) 374.

21. Kristeva, 23–24.

22. Kristeva, 25–26.

23. Kristeva, 28.

24. Kristeva, 29.

25. Julia Kristeva, *Powers of Horror,* trans. Leon S. Roudiez (New York: Columbia University Press, 1982) 24.

26. Kristeva, *Tales of Love* 37.

27. Kristeva, *Tales of Love* 42.

28. Kristeva, *Tales of Love* 43.

29. Kristeva, *Powers of Horror* 5–6.

30. Kristeva, *Powers of Horror* 39.

31. Kristeva, *Powers of Horror* 54.

32. Kristeva, *Powers of Horror* 58.

33. Kristeva, *Powers of Horror* 64.

34. Kristeva, *Powers of Horror* 62–63.

35. Kristeva, *Powers of Horror* 65.

36. Kristeva, *Powers of Horror* 73.

37. Kristeva, *Powers of Horror* 73.

38. Kristeva, *Powers of Horror* 82.

39. Kristeva, *Powers of Horror* 82.

40. Kristeva, *Powers of Horror* 74.

41. Kristeva, *Powers of Horror* 71.

42. Kristeva, *Powers of Horror* 76.

43. Kristeva, *Powers of Horror* 100.

44. Kristeva, *Powers of Horror* 111.

45. Kristeva, *Powers of Horror* 113.

46. Kristeva, *Powers of Horror* 116.

47. Kristeva, *Powers of Horror* 116.

48. Kristeva, *Powers of Horror* 117.

49. Kristeva, *Powers of Horror* 118.

50. Kristeva, *Powers of Horror* 119.

51. Kristeva, *Powers of Horror* 127.

52. See Rudolph M. Bell, *Holy Anorexia* (Chicago: University of Chicago Press, 1985).

53. Kristeva, *Powers of Horror* 129.

54. Kristeva, *Powers of Horror* 208–209.

55. Kristeva, *Powers of Horror* 55.

56. Kristeva, *Powers of Horror* 77.

57. Kristeva, *Tales of Love* 46.

58. Kristeva, *Tales of Love* 382.

Martha Reineke's essay brings together the issues of narcissism, of sacrifice, of abjection. She begins with an examination of René Girard's *Violence and the Sacred*, attending to the triadic construction of the subject as Girard presents it, and to the way in which this underlies the sacrificial constitution of social existence. She proceeds to show the closeness of the parallel between Girard's account and Kristeva's, with the key difference that Kristeva specifies the gendered character of the archaic members of the triad (parents and infant). Reineke underscores the fact that, corresponding to his neglect of gender in his account of the foundations of self and society, Girard has neglected the gender of sacrificial victims and scapegoats — characteristically women in Girard's own accounts, though he does not comment on the fact. She draws on Kristeva's analysis of abjection to account for this, and emphasizes in conclusion that collapsing the triad into a dyad, which is for Girard an essential moment, is for Kristeva a breakdown of the core structure of the subject.

In the course of this specialized discussion of Kristeva and Girard, Reineke manages to interact fruitfully with each of the other essays in this volume. Jonte-Pace's concern about the way in which religion and the feminine are associated in a screen over issues of difference and death is focused in this analysis through the role of the archaic mother as original matrix of both separation and violence. Society is founded on that separation and violence; religion sustains it, ritually and sacrificially. It may be sublimated, but not simply omitted. Edelstein's essay notes the criticism made by some feminists against Kristeva's central attention to the question of the mother (fearing that it perpetuates a patriarchal stereotype; fearing also that it threatens to expose a negation intrinsic to their own identity?). If Reineke is right, the centrality of mother in the violence that founds society underlies the whole problematic of victimization and abjection of women, and its omission would leave unexamined a central key to the relation between gender and negativity.

I have already discussed my own interaction with Reineke's essay. Fisher proposes to develop a postmodern ethics for which a split, Kristevan subject rooted in the maternal, somatic *chora* is the actor, and for which ethics is understood as a signifying practice. But if social coexistence is founded on violence, if the subject is not only split but empty at the core and the maternal *chora* a semiotic residue of what is irrevocably lost, is such an ethics possible? If so, at least it must be imbedded in questions of gender, in questions of the mimetic and the triadic, in the violent foundations of signification, thus of signifying practices ethical or not.

Kearns explores the centrality of imagination, of the fictive, of *écriture*, and the possibilities for religious play and for prayer in the space of imagination. Is this, too, darkened and bound by the violence of origins? or is Kearns's invocation of Thomas Aquinas's teleological approach relevant here — in the sense that, however divided our origins may be, imagination or fiction can construct a unifying future through a willing semiotic disruption of the symbolic that is at the same time a symbolic relativization of the archaic energies of the semiotic? May one, in other words, transcend the Girard-Kristeva problematic in the company of the later and more polymorphous Kristeva? This question also extends to Graybeal's essay, for the question of *balanse*, of *jouissance*, of joying in the life of self-division is also a question of moving beyond the dark and archaic toward the open, the possible, the plural and playful.

I want to take up for comment two other issues from Reineke's essay. Girard holds that in Christianity the death of Jesus becomes the decisive sacrifice, the substitute and scapegoat by which the community's need for representation of its founding violence is displaced outside the living community altogether. If the archaic root of that violence is maternal, evoking the scapegoating of women, can this substitution of the Son be maintained, and how? If not, what alternative understanding of the sacrificial motif in Christology might derive from the Kristevan analysis, and how would it affect the possibilities for a more effective displacement of the founding violence into the symbolic?

Reineke raises toward the end of her essay the question of whether the persistence of the violence of our social and personal origins portends catastrophe. Do we approach carnival or apocalypse? If, with Graybeal, we dance, do we dance on top of a volcano? Jonte-Pace and Reineke both find the landscape darkening as they pursue their analysis. Perhaps Fisher and Crownfield and maybe Edelstein seek to neutralize the darkness in the symbolic universality of scholarly discourse.

Reineke herself turns, in her conclusion, toward the later, con-structive side of Kristeva. Locating the paternal archaically in the ima-ginary, rendering fictive its symbolic universality (I would say), might free the imaginary from paternal tyranny and empower it to the subli-matory functions noted in Crownfield and the jubilatory ones of Gray-beal, "counter[ing] the tragic dynamics of a sacrificial economy with a promise of love as 'the builder of spoken spaces.' "

# 5

# KRISTEVA'S CHORA AND THE SUBJECT OF POSTMODERN ETHICS

### David Fisher

*David Fisher's is the only one of our essays to focus primarily on Kristeva's most theoretical work,* Revolution in Poetic Language. *A philosophical ethicist trained in theology, Fisher is concerned about what postmodern deconstruction of the subject does to the problem of ethics. If the subject (which must mean also the subject of moral action) is divided, barred, fictive, other to itself, how is anything like ethics possible?*

### *PREBODY*

when god lets my body be

From each brave eye shall sprout a tree
fruit that dangles therefrom

the purpled world will dance upon
Between my lips which did sing

a rose shall beget the spring
that maidens whom passion wastes

will lay between their little breasts
My strong fingers beneath the snow

Into strenuous birds shall go
my love walking in the grass

their wings will touch with her face
and all the while my heart shall be

With the bulge and nuzzle of the sea

e.e. cummings *(Tulips and Chimneys)*

*Now, if a contemporary ethics is no longer seen as being the same as morality;
if ethics amounts to not avoiding the embarrassing and inevitable problematics
of the law but giving it flesh, language,* jouissance *— in that case its reformulation demands the contribution of women.*

"Stabat Mater" (Kristeva Reader 185)

*I . . . argue in favor of an analytical theory of signifying systems and practices
that would search within signifying phenomena for the* crisis *of the* unsettling *process of meaning and subject rather than for the coherence or identity
or either* one *or a* multiplicity *of structures.*

"From One Identity to An Other" (Desire in Language 125)

### 1. KRISTEVA AND POSTMODERN ETHICS:
### UNSETTLING GROUNDING

Julia Kristeva's rethinking of ethics as a signifying practice rather than
as a foundational basis for morality makes a substantial contribution to
development of a postmodern ethic. A central part of that contribution
is her account of the difficult birth of divided subjects out of the maternal womb of the semiotic *chora* into the symbolic space of language and
culture, governed by the "Law of the Father" (Lacan). Fear of the archaic mother's generative power as the power that orders the *chora* is
seen as the source of attempts to control women's place in society and
of a rejection of the subject's link to body. Discussing the phenomenology of defilement in *Powers of Horror,* Kristeva argues that

> defilement reveals, at the same time as an attempt to throttle ma-
> trilineality, an attempt at separating the speaking being from his
> body in order that the latter accede to the status of clean and
> proper body, that is to say, non-assimilable, uneatable, abject. . . .
> Fear of the uncontrollable generative mother repels me from the
> body; I gave up cannibalism because abjection (of the mother)
> leads me toward respect for the body of the other, my fellow man,
> my brother (*Powers of Horror* 78–79).

To appreciate the implications of Kristeva's work for postmodern
ethics, one must begin by noting the contrast between her understanding of ethics as the "negativizing of narcissism within a practice" (RPL
233) and the self-imposed foundational task of modern philosophical

ethics. This was the task of constructing a philosophical anthropology to serve as a rational basis for morality when tradition and transcendence were undermined by Enlightenment critical thought. The moral subject was understood as a bounded and unified agent of action framed by goals. These goals, and the moral worth of the agent's actions in promoting them, were to be preserved against a background of heterogeneous impulses. Only when this primary task of defending a central self against an inner, irrational "other" had been accomplished could modern philosophical ethics proceed to its other major task of providing a rational basis for a social contract: defining the interests that a unified subject must protect in relation to others. Characterization of the "other," the rejected unconscious, driven, archaic, heterogeneous subject, was seen as an unnecessary task for moral philosophy.

In an emerging postmodern perspective on ethics informed by psychoanalysis, an understanding of the relationship between the divided subject and the imagination of moral identity has begun to change the questions addressed by normative ethics. There has been a reaction against an archaeology of the disembodied subject of consciousness (as articulated by the epistemological tradition from Descartes to Kant) as the starting point for moral reflection, and growing appreciation for the significance of embodiment in complex fields of experience and practices.

This embodiment has been represented in contrasting ways by the literatures of phenomenology and poststructuralism. There is the experiential embodiment of subjects in the phenomenological sense of lived bodies—an embodiment that is subject of and subject to the flesh of others through touch, the caress.[1] There is also an intertextual embodiment of subjects inscribed within chains of differential signifiers and sounds. This second sense of embodiment, figural and allusive, is an important source for Kristeva's account of signifying practices.

As Kristeva depicts signifying practices, these symbolic activities are founded upon prior semiotic heterogeneity: "no sign, no predication, no signified object and therefore no operating consciousness of a transcendental ego" (*Desire in Language* 133) is indispensable. Responding to both senses of embodiment, the major question for a postmodern ethic is no longer the possibility of a transcendent or transcendental foundation for moral practices. The problem is rather discerning how embodied subjects of desire emerge from complex fields of difference and how this difference shapes ethics as a signifying practice.

Fields of difference occur in gaps between heterogeneous processes and differentiating signifying practices. While not directed to ethicists as such, Kristeva's work, building on Lacan's distinction between imaginary and symbolic but "grounding" the imaginary in an abject, archaic mother image, offers a helpful way to depict the subject's initial dispersal within the imaginary order and its subsequent "birth" in the symbolic. Her discussion of the origins of desiring subjects in heterogeneous processes of the semiotic *chora*, and the origins of speaking subjects in signifying practices within the symbolic order, offers ethicists a way to grasp what is absent from classical modernist arguments about the subject of ethics: recognition of the semiotic force of the subject's origins in an abject maternal body and recognition of the need for ethics as a signifying practice to respond to the resultant material contradictions within the subject. The following remarks accordingly begin with an explication of Kristeva's distinction between semiotic process and signifying practice. This is followed by discussion of the semiotic *chora* as the heterogeneous process from which subjects emerge and a summary of her depiction of the abject maternal body image as the ordering principle of the *chora*. The essay concludes with programmatic suggestions for postmodern ethics in the light of these Kristevan concepts.

## 2. THE COMPLEXITY OF PRACTICE

I shall call signifying practice the establishment and countervailing of a sign system. Establishing a sign system calls for the identity of a speaking subject within a social framework, which he recognizes as a basis for that identity. Countervailing the sign system is done by having the subject undergo an unsettling, questionable process; this indirectly challenges the social framework with which he had previously identified, and it thus coincided with times of abrupt changes, renewal, or revolution in society. (*Desire in Language* 18)

Kristeva's nonteleological account of "signifying practice" develops from a Hegelian-Marxist understanding of practice in a form that deconstructs its archeteleological character: maintaining difference between origin and destiny means abandoning the dream of linking beginning and end that has haunted Western thought since Aristotle. As Richard Bernstein suggests, Hegel preserves the Aristotelian tradition of a fundamental unity between beginning and end through the notion that all is *aufgehoben* in the universal activity of Geist:

*Geist* as activity itself is *praxis*. *Theoria*, in its purest form as philosophy, is nothing but the articulation of the rationality ingredient in *praxis*. There is then an ultimate harmony of theory and practice . . . not in the sense that philosophy guides action but rather in the sense the philosophy is the comprehension of what is. . . . Marx *accepts* this unity of *theoria* and *praxis* and dialetically transforms it. . . . [2]

For Marx *praxis* is a critical alternative to Hegel's Geist in which a complex body of meanings—including "production, labor, alienation, relentless criticism and revolutionary practice are aspects of a single, comprehensive and coherent theory of man and his world."[3] Yet in spite of Marx's intent to emphasize sensuous human activity in opposition to Hegel's idealism, Marx's materialism remains teleological:

not in the sense that teleology commits us to the fantastic notion that a final cause precedes in time an actual event and somehow directs it, but in the empirical sense of teleology where we want to distinguish goal-directed activity from the mechanical regularity of matter in motion. Even where Marx is most explicit about his materialism—in *Capital*—he characterizes human activity in the form of labor as directed by *purposes*.[4]

For Kristeva, by contrast, understanding ethics as "the negativizing of narcissism within a *practice*" (RPL, 233) involves a nonteleological positing *and* dissolving of the meaning and the unity of the subject.

the notion of *practice* . . . would be applied to texts in which heterogeneous contradiction is maintained as an indispensable precondition for the dimensions of practice through a signifying formation . . . The fundamental moment of practice is the heterogeneous contradiction that posits a subject put in process/on trial by a natural or social outside that is not yet symbolized, a subject in conflict with previous theses . . . The subject of this experience-in-practice is an excess, never one, always already divided . . . (*Revolution in Poetic Language* 195; 203; 204)

The Kristevan notion of practice is of a human sensuous activity that introduces "material contradictions into the process of the subject" (*Revolution* 205), i.e., an activity that places the pressure of the semiotic upon the symbolic. Given this emphasis on maintaining contradiction within the subject, Kristeva is critical of Hegel and Marx. Both are "condemned to a mere repetition of actions without any modification of real, material and signifying, objective and subjective devices" because of their inability to penetrate or analyze "a null and void atomistic subjectivity."

> It is therefore incumbent upon particular signifying operations, both verbal and non-verbal, to introduce *into discourse* the analysis-in-practice that dissolves the impenetrable and atomistic subject. Otherwise, this analysis-in-practice may or may not come about as a real though always unstated contradiction in relations among atomistic subjects (*Revolution* 206–207).

An ethics based on this notion of practice would not be a positive ethic seeking to define or defend boundaries of subjects by placing them under a law or norm but an ethic of negativity closer to what Hegel calls the aesthetic than to a Kantian version of ethics as morality or to Hegel's own notion of ethics as *Sittlichkeit*. "The subject of the Hegelian aesthetic—the free subject par excellence—reveals the diremption of the ethical subject and effects its *Aufhebung* in order to reintroduce him into a process of transformation of community relations and discursive strata" (*Revolution* 110). In this way Kristeva seeks to dissolve the teleological vision of praxis/theoria unity given in the Aristotelian tradition. In her work on semiotic *chora*, she further dissolves the Platonic tradition's notion of boundaries of subjectivity established via dialectic.

### 3. CHORA'S *CLASSIC ORIGIN*; CHORA *AS THE OTHER OF SIGNIFICATION*

Kristeva is explicit about having borrowed the term *chora* to designate a mobile, unspeakable, presymbolic source of the divided subject from Plato's *Timaeus*: "We borrow the term *chora* from Plato's *Timaeus* to denote an essentially mobile and extremely provisional articulation constituted by movements and their ephemeral stases" (RPL 25). She was drawn to Plato's term by linguistic connotations of an enclosed space or womb[5] or a wet nurse, and by ambiguities present in the text of the *Timaeus*.[6] Plato makes explicit the problem she wishes to consider: the constitutive role of that which exceeds or lies beyond speech in the functioning of speech: " . . . once it has been named, that functioning, even if it is pre-symbolic, *is brought back into a symbolic position* [emphasis in original]. All discourse can do is differentiate, by means of a 'bastard reasoning,' the receptacle from motility. . . . this motility is the precondition for symbolicity, heterogeneous to it, yet indispensable" (*Revolution* 240).

The use of Plato's term has further relevance given his ambiguity about that which stands at the border between *logos* and *muthos*. His well-known rejection of poetic and rhetorical uses of language in *The Republic* and *The Sophist* is framed by his dependence upon metaphor and myth in dialectic as Derrida has shown in "White Mythology."[7] Reason is more dependent on its "other" in Platonic discourse than Plato would admit. By the use of a term first developed by Plato in the context of his patriarchal "likely story about *ousia*" that seeks to colonize the unconscious, Kristeva indicates an identity-in-difference between her thought and the patriarchal ground of Western philosophy.

To be a "subject" in *any* sense is to be the product of signifying practices: that is, to be the product of language as *symbolic* structure constituted by differences between signs. But in the symbolic "The subject never *is*. The *subject* is only the *signifying process* and he appears only as a *signifying practice*, that is, only when he is absent *within the position* out of which social, historical, and signifying activity unfolds. There is no science of the subject" (*Revolution* 215). The prior location of the subject is in processes that cannot be named, not in signifying operations from which the subject as process is always absent.

The identity/nonidentity of subject as signifying process exists prior to "birth" into the symbolic order of language under the "Father's law." This primary subject of desire emerges from the division between "need" and "demand" within a semiotic chain of images "structured *like* a language" that underlies the symbolic order. Derrida, in his debate with Lacan, has argued that there is nothing outside of or prior to text (*il y a seulment du texte*, in the peculiar Derridean meaning of "text" as texture, *différance*, etc.[8]). By contrast with alternative psychoanalytic ways of imagining and/or deconstructing origins,[9] Kristeva like Lacan insists that language, as a structured system of regulated differences under the Father's law, can only be understood in relation to its other. This other is not a protected sphere of private identity but a complex order. There is also the "Real," the absolute other that remains unsaid and unsayable.

The *chora* is the Kristevan designation for the other of signification: the semiotic. The *chora* is therefore not a sign nor "a position that represents someone for another position (i.e., it is not a signifier)" (*Rev-*

*olution* 26). It is rather "a modality of significance in which the linguistic sign is not yet articulated as the absence of an object and as the distinction between real and symbolic (RPL 26). She compares the *chora* to Melanie Klein's "pre-Oedipal" stage of human development. This is the stage before the subject's "discovery" of castration anxiety and the positing of the superego. Kristeva's view of this stage

> "is as follows: Without 'believing' or 'desiring' any 'object' whatsoever, the subject is in the process of constituting himself vis-a-vis a non-object. He is in the process of separating from this non-object so as to make that non-object 'one' and posit himself as 'other': the mother's body is the not-yet-one that the believing and desiring subject will [subsequently] imagine as a 'receptacle.' " (*Resolution* 241, 21)

Although it is not unified, the *chora* as a functioning kinetic state "governs the connections between the body (in the process of constituting itself as the body proper), objects, and protagonists of the family structure" (*Resolution* 27). The mother's body is the ordering principle of the *chora*, since speaking subjects emerge into language from a background of conflict between attraction and repulsion with an image of the archaic mother. This maternal body image is formed as the result of a major transposition. The fragmentary subject of early infancy, confronted with an idealized image of itself (given in an actual mirror or the "mirroring" gaze of another person), confirms the attractiveness and power of that "perfect" image and then — fatally — identifies its "true self" *as* that image; it seeks to be "other" than it is; in Lacan's words to "come to be in a 'place' where 'it' is not." The subject that emerges from this unnameable point of division is a split subject, identifying its previous, fragmentary experience with the source of life, imagined as the mother's body. Because the maternal body is experienced as *both* the originating, nurturing source of subjectivity (hence desired) *and* rejected as abject or horrifying in light of the "perfect" image that the subject now wishes to become, the maternal image is at once a source of fascination and rejection.

Kristeva summarizes the ambiguity of *chora* when she states that "the semiotic chora is no more than the place where the subject is both generated and negated, the place where his unity succumbs before the process of charges and stases that produce him. We shall call this process of charges and stases a *negativity* to distinguish it from negation, which is the act of a judging subject" (*Revolution* 28). While the speaking subject, as the product of signifying practices in the symbolic order, may gain identity from a specific location, this location is seen in relation to the *chora* to have been the product of prior relationships between presymbolic elements.

## 4. THE ABJECT MATERNAL BODY AS THE ORDERING PRINCIPLE OF THE CHORA

The maternal body that functions as the ordering principle of the *chora* is not identifiable as the body of an individual human (or — superhuman) subject.

> . . . the maternal body is the place of a splitting. Through a body destined to insure reproduction of the species, the woman-subject . . . [is] more of a filter than anyone else— a thoroughfare, a threshold where 'nature' confronts 'culture.' To imagine that there is *someone* in that filter — such is the source of religious mystifications. (*Desire in Language* 238)

As this "place" that is not a place (since "it" lacks location within the system of signifying differences), the maternal preobject/abject is unnameable; "present" only as image. When a speaking subject, male or female, confronts this unnameable entity it confronts the most archaic 'object'

> still inseparable from drives. The abject is that pseudo-object that is made up *before* but appears only *within* the gaps of secondary repression . . . The abject confronts us . . . with our earliest attempts to release the hold of maternal entity, even before ex-isting outside of her. . . . The more or less beautiful image in which I behold or recognize myself rests upon an abjection that sunders it as soon as repression, the constant watchman, is relaxed. (*Powers of Horror* 13)

In *Powers of Horror* Kristeva finds traces of this abject in incest taboos of "primitive" cultures. Incest dread responds to elements experienced as beyond all cultural boundaries. These elements threaten the structure of symbolic order since they undermine its absolute, taken-for-granted character by indicating something more primordial, something that can not be represented within cultural schemes of binary op-

positions (i.e., raw/cooked, clean/defiled, sacred/profane). Such elements include excrement and its equivalents, representing dangers to
identity from *without* (ego threatened by the non-ego), and menstrual
blood, representing danger issuing from identities established *within*
the social/sexual order. Arguing that both "defilements" stem from the
maternal and/or feminine, Kristeva further noes the prelinguistic immersion of all subjects in a specific process of maternal authority: oral
frustration and sphincteral training. The resulting repulsion/attraction
toward the imaged maternal body is powerful:

> devotees of the abject, she as well as he, do not cease looking,
> within what flows from the other's 'innermost being' for the desir-
> able and terrifying, nourishing and murderous, fascinating and
> abject inside of the maternal body. (*Powers of Horror* 54)

Language, which enables a subject to differentiate itself from the other,
does so by repressing archaic maternal authority prior to language, an
authority that had developed a semiotic or presymbolic mapping of the
"self's clean and proper body." Before all strictures of morality en-
crypted in language there is a "pre-thetic" power that sets limits on motility and expression of drives.

   None of this account of presymbolic origins denies the differentiating power of culture, social structure, or economic class in the subsequent construction of bodies within signifying practices. What Kristeva is claiming is that an identifiable subject, locatable within systems
of signification, presupposes a heterogeneous, unpositioned subject
determined by repressed and horrifying powers of the maternal body.
This means that the mind-body split that has shaped so much modern
ethical thought is based on repression of body and body processes connected to an abject maternal body.

## 5. CONCLUSION AND CODA: KRISTEVA AND
## POSTMODERN ETHICS

Kristeva has suggested some possibilities for postmodern ethics in two
recent texts, *In the Beginning Was Love: Psychoanalysis and Faith* and *Tales
of Love*,[10] but discussion of these possibilities linked as they are to details
of psychoanalytic practice, narrative, and an archeology of love, extend
beyond the scope of these remarks on the relation between ethics as a
signifying practice and the relation of that practice to the semiotic *chora*.

Within these limits, however, three points can be proposed in relation to postmodern ethics.

First, Kristeva's work challenges *autonomy and principle* as the ground for morality by calling attention to the subject's emerging from while remaining attached to its origins in the heterogeneous materiality of the *chora*. To think rational autonomy as the essential ground of ethics is to repress the abject origin of images within the *chora* from which subjects emerge. To put the matter in other terms, Kristeva's development of the "split subject" through specific images of horror underlines the inevitability/instability of the subject's division. One can not think ethics as a reflective practice apart from such heterogeneous images, and to think heterogeneous images is to think otherwise than in terms of the autonomy of atomistic subjects, achieved under unifying principles.

A second implication of Kristeva's work challenges some themes prominent in recent Christian ethics. Calling attention to the primacy of a synchronic system of conflicting images at the origin of subjects rather than positing an ideal of hoped-for transcendent, eschatological unity as the basic "text" for ethical reflection, she undermines notions of responsibility and hope as these have been developed in Christian ethics. Responding to the erosion of identity, by historical relativism, contextualist Christian ethics argued for a discernment of God's originary action upon the self as the main basis for moral identity. More recently, theologies of hope and theologies of story have been turned to the self's destiny rather than its beginning; to promised visions of *jouissance* for divided selves in eschatological, communitarian forms of identity. The narrative character of religious ethics in particular has led some religious ethicists to see narrative closure as an ideal, diachronic representation of ultimate synchronic or atemporal unity.

From the Kristevan perspective on the *chora*, trust in an aboriginal unity of the subject given in God's action, or hope for eschatological unity with other selves at the completion of "herstory" must equally be viewed as instances of traditional Christian polemic against the disturbing power of heterogeneous images in the name of the one God and unified subject; a polemic based on rejection of the heterogeneity of origins that the *chora* implies, as well as on rejection of the open, anti-closural character of signifying practices that heterogeneous roots suggest. As exhibited in various genealogies of struggle between iconic and aniconic traditions from ancient Israel through Puritanism, this rejection, as Kristeva suggests in some detail in *Powers of Horror*, represents a patriarchal reaction against the power of the abject. In the Judeo-Christian imagination, this abject power has been first projected onto "evil" or "static" goddess images, only in order to be "overcome" by an eschatological victory of light and order, of *lux perpetua* over darkness, the Patriarchal Word and light triumphant over Maternal image and darkness. To the extent that one assumes the divided origins of subjects within the semiotic *chora*, hopes for eternal *jouissance* are forms of defensive identification with an ego ideal against the maternal image, or identification with the superego as the "Father's Law."

Third, to the extent that Kristeva's work deconstructs the possibility of positive identification with the maternal body as much as it challenges identification with the Father's law, her work questions the essentialism present in some recent feminist religious ethics based upon memories and dreams of the Goddess,[11] or on the practices that seek to create intersubjective space through positive/empowering images of the Goddess. In "Women's Time," Kristeva makes the challenge explicit:

> If the archetype of the belief in a good and pure substance, that of utopias, is the belief in the omnipotence of an archaic, full, total, englobing mother with no frustrations, no separation, with no break-producing symbolism (with no castration, in other words), then it becomes evident that we will never be able to defuse the violences mobilized through the counterinvestment necessary to carrying out this phantasm, unless one challenges precisely this myth of the archaic mother. (*Kristeva Reader* 205)

Kristeva proposes, in contrast, the need for a "third stage" of feminism. Such a "third stage" would understand previous feminist thinking — thinking that characterizes the man/woman dichotomy as an oppositional relationship between two rival entities — as belonging to "metaphysics." A new feminist ethic at once declares its adherents guilty, while immediately affording them the possibility for *jouissance* — unbounded joy or ecstasy. It is a question — *contra* Kierkegaard — of seeing ethical signifying practices as both/and, not as either/or. Kristeva is not questioning whether it is possible, or in some sociopolitical contexts necessary, to seek positive feminine images through practices of mutual care, or to identify one's fragmented self with such images in order to promote healing and closure. It is rather a question of remembering the limitations inherent in any *ethical* signifying practice (i.e., in a practice dedicated to maintaining contradictions), when dealing with the heterogeneity of the *chora* from which signifying practices emerges.

The preceding remarks have indicated some issues with which a postmodern ethical reflection could begin. Kristeva's work, to the extent that it reinforces and expands the Lacanian emphasis on a divided subject, undermines classical and modern ethical concepts of subjective unity as the ground of moral agency. Her work can be best understood as an admonition to ethicists to recall the inchoate, complex beings of moral reflection against which specific figures of moral identity, moral community, and moral ends emerge. Moral reflection requires *both* figure and ground since it is the tension between them that moves the process of reflection from initial contrasts to forms of practical analysis leading to open yet decisive action.

The need for this figure/ground tension in moral reflection is similar to poetry's need for figure and ground, as Wallace Stevens presents it in "The Rock." Stevens's bright, dry, images serve as both complement and contrast to the darker, mustier images of horror summoned forth by Kristeva:

> It is not enough to cover the rock with leaves.
> We must be cured of it by a cure of the ground
> Or a cure of ourselves, that is equal to a cure
>
> Of the ground, a cure beyond forgetfulness.
> And yet the leaves, if they broke into bud,
> If they broke into bloom, if they bore fruit,
>
> And we ate the incipient colorings
> Of their fresh culls might be a cure of the ground.
> The fiction of the leaves is the icon
>
> Of the poem, the figuration of blessedness,
> And the icon is the man. The pearled chaplet of
>     spring,
> The magnum wreath of summer, time's autumn
>     snood,
>
> Its copy of the sun, these cover the rock.
> These leaves are the poem, the icon and the man.
> They are a cure of the ground and of ourselves,
>
> In the predicate that there is nothing else.[12]

The "cure"—both for psychoanalysis and for Stevens in this poem—is at once cure and the disease; or rather, the cure occurs within an imagination of the space between disease and cure. Understood in postmodern perspective ethics is at once a "cure" of wounds experienced in differentiation from the *chora* and a disease that multiplies those wounds to excess since a postmodern ethic dissolves attempts to achieve the final identity of a "pure" moral agent or self as an illusion.

One does not resolve moral dilemmas by identifying the ideal self with pure practical reason (Kant); with the higher pleasures that support the common good (Mill); with a telos tacitly given by moral tradition (Aristotle/MacIntyre); or by self-identification with a constructed ideal of reflective equilibrium of interests (Rawls).

A "cure of ourselves equal to a cure of the ground" is said to be beyond forgetfulness; not in the sense of abolishing memories, but in the sense of following after images, after fictions produced as icons by painful memory in the "predicate that there is nothing else." No resolution of contrasts, only an experience of the contrasts in the supreme fiction that is poetry—akin to the signifying practice of ethics. Or, as Kristeva suggests, the complex contrasts of images in the *chora* are not to be resolved in the sense that traditional moral dilemmas demand resolution; they are to be worked through in the sense implied by Stevens's poem. The depiction of this process of ethical "working through," of a "cure" beyond archeological or teleological identity, is a task made urgent by Kristeva's work but one standing beyond the limits of the present discussion.

## NOTES

1. Maurice Merleau-Ponty, *The Visible and the Invisible,* trans. Alphonso Lingis (Evanston: Northwestern University Press, 1966).

2. Richard J. Bernstein, *Praxis and Action* (Philadelphia: University of Pennsylvania Press, 1971), 34. See Guy Planty-Bonjour, "Hegel's Concept of Action As Unity of Poiesis and Praxis," in *Hegel's Philosophy of Action,* eds. Lawrence S. Stepelevich and David Lamb (Atlantic Highlands: Humanities Press, 1983) 19–29, for comparison of Aristotle and Hegel's differing understandings of the theoria-praxis-poiesis relationship. Recent discussion of practice in American ethics has focused on Alasdair MacIntyre's teleological definition of practice in relation to "narrative of a whole life" and a moral tradition in *After Virtue* (2nd ed.; Notre Dame: University of Notre Dame Press, 1984) in contrast to the constructivist idea of practice offered by John Rawls in *A Theory of Justice* (Cambridge, Mass: Harvard University Press, 1971), and Michael Walzer's quasi-communitarian account in *Spheres of Justice: A Defense of Pluralism and Equality (New York: Basic Books, 1983)*. This ethical literature does not respond to Reiner Schurmann's "raising the inherited question of the relationship between theory and practice . . . considered under Heidegger's hypothesis that metaphysical rationality produced its own closure," in Reiner Schurmann, *Heidegger on Being and Acting: From Principles to Anarchy,* trans. Christine-Marie Gros (Bloomington: Indiana University Press, 1987). Kristeva's "signifying practice"

offers a unique perspective that remains to be integrated with this larger body of literature.

3. Bernstein, 76.

4. Bernstein, 42–43.

5. This point is suggested by Toril Moi in her introduction to *The Kristeva Reader, op. cit.*, 12.

6. She says:
Plato emphasizes that the receptacle (ὑποδοχεῖον) which is also called space (χώρα) vis-à-vis reason, is necessary—but not divine since it is unstable, uncertain, ever changing and becoming; it is unnameable, improbable, bastard. . . . Is the receptacle a 'thing' or a mode of language? Plato's hesitation between the two gives the receptacle an even more uncertain status. It is one of the elements that antedate not only the universe but also names and even syllables. . . . On the one hand, the receptacle is mobile and even contradictory, without unity, separable and divisible: pre-syllable, pre-word. Yet, on the other hand, because this separability and divisibility antecede numbers and forms, the space of the receptacle is called *amorphous;* thus its suggested rhythmicity will in a certain sense be erased, for how can one think an articulation of what is not yet singular but is nevertheless necessary? (*Revolution in Poetic Language* 239: Ns. 12, 13)

7. Jacques Derrida, "White Mythology: Metaphor in the Text of Philosophy," in Jacques Derrida, *Margins of Philosophy*, trans. with additional notes by Alan Bass (Chicago: University of Chicago Press, 1982) 207–27. Kristeva's own position on metaphor is complex, occupying a place between Derrida's poststructural deconstruction of subjectivity (criticized by Kristeva in "From One Identity to An Other," *Desire in Language* 124–147: 131), and Paul Ricoeur's phenomenological argument for the bounded subject in response to Derrida (in "Metaphor and Philosophical Discourse," in *The Rule of Metaphor*, trans. Robert Czerny with Kathleen McLaughlin and John Costello, S. J. (Toronto: University of Toronto Press, 1977) 257–313.)

8. For Derrida "*Text*, as I use the word, is not the book. . . . It is precisely for strategic reasons. . . . that I found it necessary to recast the concept of text by generalizing it almost without limit, in any case without present or perceptible limit, without any limit that *is*." Cited by Bill Readings in "The Deconstruction of Politics," n. 13, p. 240, in *Reading De Man Reading*, eds. Lindsay Walters & Wlad Godzich (Minneapolis: University of Minnesota Press, 1989. For Kristeva's different understanding of text see "The Bounded Text" in *DL* 36–63: "the *text* is a trans-linguistic apparatus that redistributes the order of language by relating communicative speech, which aims to inform directly, to different kinds of anterior or synchronic processes. The *text* is therefore a *productivity*, and this means: first, that its relationship to the language in which it is situated

is redistributive (deconstructive-constructive), and hence can be better approached through logical categories than linguistic ones; and second, that it is a permutation of texts, an intertextuality: in the space of a given text, several utterances, taken from other texts, intersect and neutralize each other." The split subject is an "intertext" for Kristeva in the sense that it always combines the semiotic "pre-text" of the *chora* with symbolic texts of signifying practices within which speaking subjects are situated.

9. For an account of the "original mental state" of newborn infants viewed within a range of psychodynamic theories other than those of Lacan or Kristeva, see Victoria Hamilton, *Narcissus and Oedipus: The Children of Psychoanalysis* (London: Routledge & Kegan Paul, 1982). See also Juliet Mitchell's sharply critical response to Hamilton from a Lacanian feminist perspective in *Women: The Longest Revolution* (New York: Random House, 1984), 278–86.

10. *In the Beginning Was Love: Psychoanalysis and Faith*, trans. Arthur Goldhammer (New York: Columbia University Press, 1987) and *Tales of Love*, trans. Leon S. Roudiez (New York: Columbia University Press, 1987).

11. See, for example, Joan Chamberlain Engelsman, *The Feminine Dimension of the Divine* (Philadelphia: Westminster Press, 1979).

12. Wallace Stevens, *The Collected Poems of Wallace Stevens* (New York: Alfred A. Knopf, 1977) 526–527. The figure-ground relationship invoked by Stevens continues to play a central role in contemporary American poetry's attempt to deal with the "death" of the closed, foundational modernist subject. In "But What Is the Reader to Make of This?" John Ashbery parodies Stevens' image of a cure of the leaf-covered ground:

Meanwhile the combinations of every extendable circumstance
In our lives continue to blow against it like new leaves
At the edge of a forest a battle rages in and out of
For a whole day. It's not the background, we're the background,
On the outside looking out.

John Ashbery, *A Wave.* (New York: Viking Press, 1981)

# INTER-TEXT 5

What does it mean for Fisher, or for Kristeva, to speak of ethics as a "signifying practice?" Neither of them seems to make it fully explicit, and the possibility of a postmodern ethics depends, if Fisher is right, on clarifying it.

In general, Kristeva means by "signifying practice" the establishing and countervailing (unsettling, questioning, challenging) of a sign system that inscribes an identity for an individual within a social framework (DL 18). She also defines ethics as "the negativizing of narcissism within a practice" (RPL 233). To call ethics a signifying practice thus seems to be to identify it as the establishment and enactment of a sign system that inscribes a non-narcissistic identity, or troubles a narcissistic one, within a social framework. As Fisher points out, this displaces traditional sorts of ethics that seek a rational (or, in theology, revealed) foundation for morality. The issue becomes no longer what should we do, but how shall we publicly inscribe the identity of the acting individual in a non-narcissistic way?

Fisher develops this problematic in relation to the problem of the divided self: the inner heterogeneity of desire, of body, of unconscious drive. If Lacan's claim is right, that the (agent) subject of our action and discourse is unconscious, that the ego we identify as "I" in our discourse — and the unitive subject it purports to be — is imaginary, what follows for ethics? The focus shifts from rational claims on the ego to the inscribing, the socializing, the positioning of the (unconscious, non-unified) subject in public discourse and practice. Ego is then at best a signifier barred from its signified like any other, implicated in the relativity, the arbitrariness, the open-ended play of displacements and differences that constantly unsettles the materials of signification. As the (unconscious, non-unified) subject enters through practice into the public world, the discursive mappings within which ego is located ascribe an identity and public location to it and thus participate in configuring that practice. What sorts of discourse about subjects and about practices configure ego and practice in a negation of narcissism, an openness to the other?

In Kristeva, as Fisher tells us, the primordial matrix of divided subjectivity is the *chora:* the space of inscription of archaic experiences of difference, from birth to nourishment, pain, relief, absence, motility, which are preconditions for signifying representations. The archaic differences by which practice is configured lie here, before the articulations of the symbolic. The subject, generated from this matrix, is the signifying activity itself, always absent from the text of signification as well as from its maternal matrix, dissociated from the somatic activity that is its own generation. The Real, as body, as separation, as the sensuous contradictions integral to practice, is the Other of signifying practice, unsayable even as it is the requisite of signification. The *chora* is a retrospectively imagined container that precedes the distinction of mother, self and object, and of real and symbolic.

As we saw in Reineke, the emergence of a subjectivity from this matrix involves fundamental negativity, abjection. Trace of mother's body, of violent separation, of negation and loss, the matrix is the object of abhorrence and rage. Discourse of the "clean and proper body" represses this negation and obscures the inherent negativity of the subject. Ethics, as signifying practice, must then reinscribe this subject identity in a way that sublimates its negativity: through sacrifice or purification, as Reineke discusses, or through construction of a relational signifying practice that can displace the narcissistic dyad of mother and child and open a space for self-being that neither destroys nor is destroyed by the other — as both Crownfield and Reineke have considered.

Fisher's conclusion affirms Kristeva against ethical appeals to principle or to autonomy and against theological models of the unified subject either aboriginally derived from God's action or teleologically ordered by eschatological expectation. He appropriately notes the illusory, defensive, and patriarchal character of these models and appeals. He ends by quoting Wallace Stevens' "The Rock," with its image of "a cure of ourselves, that is equal to / / a cure of the ground." In ending with a poem, Fisher exemplifies what his analysis does not make explicit: the possibility of fictive, optional, poetic models. What is the import for ethics of inscribing ourselves in an imaginary discourse, in pluralities of images and fictions and playings?

Kearns and Graybeal (reflecting their attention to materials that develop later in Kristeva's work) both find this move to the fictive central to the appropriation of Kristeva. Crownfield, along with Kearns (and Reineke, too, in her conclusion), propose that the religious discourse of the tradition may itself be understood fictively, and continue to be in play in the relativizing, the sublimating, the negativizing of narcissism within a practice.

This displacement of the problematic of ethics depends on Kristeva's notion of practice. As Fisher shows us, practice is for her sensuous activity, engaged with a natural or social outside that exceeds, defies, differs from the system of signification, and thus introduces material contradictions into the process of the subject. Hegel and Marx, she holds, fail to achieve an adequate notion of practice in that they assume an atomistic subjectivity, failing to recognize the existence of heterogeneity (both sensuous and spiritual [social, discursive]) within the subject, within signification, as well as within sensuous experience.

Kristeva and Fisher recognize, and I want to underscore, the extent to which signifying practice and social practices of all sorts are interembedded. Calvin Schrag, in *Communicative Praxis and the Space of Subjectivity*, develops a unitary notion of practice in which both signifying and other activities are coimplicated. The system of differences in which signification is effective includes all kinds of differences in the sensuous world, not simply the sounds and inscriptions called linguistic signifiers. Not only are linguistic acts of signification sensuous activity, but all sorts of sensuous activity participate in signification. Though Schrag does not reference Merleau-Ponty's *The Visible and the Invisible*, the comprehensive intertwining of modes of sensuous having and sensuous exposure there developed, complexified through the notion of praxis, characterizes Schrag's whole discussion.

Schrag's ethical reflection generated out of this comprehensive notion of communicative practice centers on the question of the fitting, of appropriate entry into, participation in, or refiguring of, the situation of action. But Schrag's notion of the space of subjectivity, while informed by Kierkegaard, Heidegger, and even Derrida, remains relatively free of the more severely problematizing challenges of Nietzsche, Freud, Lacan, and Kristeva. If subject is as radically fictive, heterogeneous, unconscious as this tradition would have it, is not the question of the fitting darkened and divided beyond utility? As Schrag's notion of communicative practice helps clarify Fisher's discussion of a postmodern ethics as signifying practice, so also Fisher's, and Kristeva's, more radical critique of the subject might problematize, and eventually enrich, Schrag's discussion.

# 6

# ART AND RELIGIOUS DISCOURSE IN AQUINAS AND KRISTEVA

### Cleo McNelly Kearns

*For a wide range of modern thinking, reality is fundamentally related to perception, and imagination implies the falsification of the real. If Kristeva were to be read in this way, her appeals to fiction and imagination would seem to support escapist illusions. That this is not the case is perhaps most illuminated by Cleo Kearns's association of Kristeva with the consummate empirical realist, Thomas Aquinas. Her indication that imagination, as a constructive synthesis of universal and particular, soul and body, is central to perception for Thomas—for realism itself—resituates talk of fiction, and talk of God, at the heart of the question of reality. The transferential value, and transferential risk, in such talk of God, and its disarming through fictive discourse, opens the space for Kearns's suggestion of a "prière feminine."*

Julia Kristeva, whose primary work is in linguistics and psychoanalysis, has also written on figures as diverse as the Virgin Mary, Duns Scotus, Thomas Aquinas, Bernard of Clairvaux, and Madame de Guyon. She has even tried her hand at Biblical exegesis, lightly enough in *Powers of Horror* and more firmly in *Tales of Love*, which contains a remarkable, if slightly baroque, reading of the *Song of Songs*. Running through this work is a profound understanding of the poetic and fantastic — she might prefer to say *phantasmatic*—nature of language, including the languages of religion and theology. Kristeva seeks, without denying their rational component or their dogmatic repressions, to recover in these languages another, more hidden, perhaps more sensual and even salvific face. While she is not at all, in almost any sense of the word, a "believer," she does insist that the recovery of this dimension of language

111

can take place only within a quasi-Christian discourse of ethics and of love.[1]

Some of the founding assumptions of Kristeva's work have a curious intersection with those of Aquinas, particularly with reference to the role of the body in religious and aesthetic apprehension and to the essential narcissism or self-valuation that founds the speaking subject. Hence a comparison between these two otherwise very disparate figures may yield some insight into both and into the issues with which they were, from such different life positions, concerned. The gap between these two figures is, of course, comically wide. Added to the obvious gulf ever fixed between the thirteenth-century celibate monastic man and the postmodern woman of letters is the explicit rejection—or at least attempted subversion—on Kristeva's part, not only of the religion to which Aquinas belongs, but of the very discourse, the discourse of theology, in which he writes. This critique, however, is by no means irrelevant to the very issues on which they jointly train their sights, so it is important to begin by understanding as precisely as possible in a short space of time why Kristeva, while speaking *about* theology and religion, does not wish to speak religiously or theologically in the usual sense.

Like other postmoderns, Kristeva approaches religion and theology with a serious hermeneutics of suspicion. Religion, for her, is at base a complex of practices and fantasies through which human beings mask from themselves the intolerable knowledge of their own mortality, and theology is primarily a rationale for that masking. As such, both have the potential to turn at any moment into the defensive, repressive, and indeed oppressive functions any such lie must at some point entail. Furthermore, theology is particularly at risk here because the kinds of claims to which it pretends lead to a deep blindness to its own nature as language, as discourse conditioned by history, by privilege, by various kinds of *partis pris*, and by that particular tone-deafness to the needs of psyche, soul, and body toward which any relentlessly rationalizing or logocentric discourse always tends.

Religion is also, however, for Kristeva a discourse, in some ways a feminine discourse, which helps to mediate, in a healing way, between the claims of law and flesh, symbolic and semiotic, order and creativity, self and other. And theology, for its part, seeks to explain, often with greater acuity than philosophy or psychoanalysis has yet achieved, how in principle and by what best strategies that healing may take place. A similar healing, without the corresponding dangers of terror and inquisition, is, Kristeva argues, available to us through art. However, we cannot rely on art mechanically nor depend automatically on its inherent qualities; we need to develop a critique of its powers and limitations as well. The history of religion and its associated theologies is full of insight for that task and warning against its dangers, including the danger, of which Kristeva is well aware, of a certain aestheticism.

To uncover the liberating potential of religion and theology involves, for Kristeva, a double critique: for religion, a psychoanalytic and for theology, a literary one. Religion, in Kristeva's terms, is a kind of systematic and highly elaborated fantasy — a "phantasmic necessity" she calls it[2] — that relieves symptoms and mediates a world to us, but that can blind us when it is taken too much for what she calls the *vréel*, the "true-real."[3] To religion, Kristeva would counterpose a free play of fantasy that does not take its images and representations for "truth," but retains an awareness of their provisional and constructed nature. Religions are made up out of language to mediate between psychological and social contradictions we cannot handle any other way.

Theology, for Kristeva, is the rationale for those fantasies, and as such it can be very acute. It, too, however, can blind when it is taken for a transparent representation of ultimate truths. To theology she would counterpose something that often goes under the name of *écriture*, writing, or poetic language. This "writing degree zero" or poetic language to which — following Roland Barthes — she gives such weight is a practice that defines itself largely over against theology and undertakes precisely to undermine its negative effects.[4] *Écriture* or writing, it is insisted, involves the self-aware, self-analytical participation in a discourse that does not pretend to rise above itself to the exalted status of pure and transparent representation of truth, but rather reveals in its own concrete, fallen, fractured, and mortal nature.

In both cases, the double critique of religion and theology through psychoanalysis and literary theory involves a full recognition that fantasy and the representation of truth both operate entirely within and are completely subject to language. (By language here is meant the broadest possible range of modalities; as when we say there is a "language of sound" in music, or a "language of form" in architecture.) If for Kristeva, religion is a form of fantasy, a phantasm that wards off death, and theology its rationale, then they can and do accomplish their ends only by making constructs out of language, and then by repressing the recognition of that material and process of manufacture. Art undoes that repression and reinstates a practice of fantasy in which our mortality and enclosure within language are not concealed but repeatedly brought to the fore.

Now Aquinas, as is well known, does not hold anything like a modern, much less postmodern view of art, which is barely discernible as a distinct human activity in much of his thought. He does have, however, as we shall see, a distinct view of fantasy and, as Umberto Eco has cogently argued, a strong theory of the nature and function of beauty. Furthermore, he works within a system that, unlike Kristeva's, sees all human activity as leading to an attainable telos involving both full recognition of the other and full unity-in-charity with the object of desire. Kristeva has no such hope; her system can only envisage a series of temporary and provisional rapprochements that inevitably lapse back toward death. Nevertheless, as she herself has recognized in *Tales of Love*, the Thomistic project, stronger on ends than on origins, frames her own, stronger on origins than on ends, in very useful and illuminating ways.

Aquinas, you may remember, insisted that the human being is a "composite," a conjuncture of soul and body, and not a duality, and that therefore we sense, understand and experience the world and our salvation not through the soul alone but through our whole mode of being, corporeal, psychological, social, and spiritual alike. Fantasy is essential to the operations of this composite and to its achievement of its goal. In several places in the *Summa*, Aquinas speaks of the imagination and of what he calls the phantasms, or *phantasmata*. He says, among other things: "In the state of the present life, in which the soul is united to a corruptible body, it is impossible for our intellect to understand anything actually, except by turning to phantasms . . . there is need for the act of the imagination and of other powers." He goes on to offer this extremely important formulation:

> The proper object of the human intellect, which is united to a body, is the quiddity or nature existing in corporeal matter; and it is through these natures of visible things that it rises to a certain knowledge of things invisible. Now it belongs to such a nature to exist in some individual, and this cannot be apart from corporeal matter . . . Now we apprehend the individual through the sense and the imagination. And, therefore, for the intellect to understand actually its proper object, it must of necessity turn to the phantasms in order to perceive the universal nature existing in the individual.[5]

By these passages I understand Aquinas to mean that the imagination and fantasy are 1) linked to somatic and physiological aspects of our being, 2) necessary for the apprehension of the universal-in-particular, the quiddity, of ourselves and of others alike.

Kristeva would entirely agree, just as she agrees with Aquinas that the basis of psychic health and even of the salvation of the soul is a deep but not unmediated self-affirmation.[6] For Aquinas, however, or so Eco argues, the point or telos of this activity of the imagination is the apprehension of the beauty of the divine and of its quiddity in the incarnate Lord.[7] Hence to separate knowledge and desire is for Aquinas an epistemological impossibility. If you cannot fantasize or imagine Christ in his particular, individual beauty, how will you know him when you see him? And by what means will you be led to desire Him? This is, in essence, Aquinas's point, and, I might add in passing, the basis of the positive cultivation of the imagination and the fantasy in the whole Ignatian project. Indeed, it governs, for good or for ill, the dominant tradition of Western meditation as well.

Kristeva too, with Aquinas, sees humans as composites, made up of an interpenetration of body and soul/psyche, or rather, in terms of her vocabulary, of semiotic and symbolic levels. (*Symbolic* here may be a misleading term for Anglo-Americans; by it Kristeva means nothing to do with symbolism in the poetical sense, but rather the rational, signifying order, the more or less logical set of codes, visual, linguistic, auditory, tactile, and legal by which we communicate with one another. By *semiotic,* she means all that cannot be coded in that way, the realm of the material, the fleshly, the instinctive, a rhythmic flux better expressed in song than in story, in color than in line, a preconscious terrain she elsewhere calls, thinking of Plato, the *chora*.[8]) She too sees fantasy and imagination as crucial in the management of that composite.

One way, among others, she differs from Aquinas, of course, is in her greater sense of the importance—the crucial and determinative importance—of language in shaping imagination and fantasy and in constructing this composite being. Language is important in Kristeva's thought because it is only through language that we enter the symbolic —the realm of law and the father, as opposed to that of the flesh and the mother—in the first place. It is language that makes us aware of the distinctions or boundaries between the self and the other, and/ or the rational I and the disruptive, dark, creative side of ourselves. Something, however, subtends that language, in both the synchronic and diachronic orders, and persists even after its acquisition. That something is the semiotic, the waves of desire and repulsion that structure the bodily, fleshly, material side of our composite nature, and that are often expressed, at the borderline between symbolic and semiotic, in fantasy.

To mention only one way in which this view may contribute to the study of religion, there is the light it casts, for Kristeva herself, on the Christian concepts of sin and penance. The tension created within and between the semiotic and the symbolic is, Kristeva argues, well-articulated in the Christian concept, phantasmatic as it may be, of sin. Christian sin is for her both the memory and the repression of the violent struggle we have undergone within the semiotic and in our attempts to move beyond it. Sin is not just an act by which we transgress the law of the father but the refusal to recognize the divided, heterogeneous, composite nature of the human mode of being. To confess sin is by definition to make that recognition and thus to overcome the repression it entailed; it is to acknowledge, "I am divided," or, to paraphrase St. Paul, "I am at war with myself." That's why, Kristeva argues, Duns Scotus was so wise to make the spoken confession, not any act of reparation that may follow it, the necessary and sufficient condition for absolution.[9]

Religion in general, as Kristeva always acknowledges, recognizes the need for semiotic involvement in our lives, especially in and through its rituals. It effects a reconcilation between the semiotic and symbolic by the creation of moments of iconicity, quasi hallucinations, fictions which blur the contradictions between true and real, spirit and body, in a plausible way. (Kristeva's analysis of the eucharist is, in this respect, a remarkable piece of theology in itself.[10]) But, for her, religious discourse continually falls back into a kind of reification. Ultimately, it strives too hard, in the name of its own version of the law and its own strategies of power, to repress or deny our recognition of materiality, language, and death.

Only art, through the controlled expression of fantasy and imagination, can for Kristeva restore us to a genuine sense of the composite human being, with his/her full mortality and desire. Only art combines awareness of the laws of communication with attention to those gaps and fissures through which we see the flesh again, but elegiacally transformed. For her art offers religion without its inquisitions, order without its fascist face, fantasy without its madness, and maternal joy without its violent and incestuous regressions. Art does better for us than religion, however, only when it recognizes its own element of *écriture*, its claim not to announce or represent an eternal truth, but to reveal, always only provisionally, the interplay between that truth and another, the truth of the material, the fleshly, the body, the here and now beneath it.

What Kristeva does to Aquinas, then, is to darken and complicate his picture of the human being by reflecting on our heterogeneous origins rather than on our unified ends. For her, the order of knowledge and the order of desire are not, as with Aquinas, so easily reconciled, because there is no Christ-point in which these parallel lines, even hypothetically, may meet. Whether in spite or because of these differences, however, her work illuminates, at least for me, not only a number of traditional Christian doctrines (original sin, the nature of law, virgin birth, incarnation, the eucharist, on all of which she has written brilliantly), but something about the mode of operation of religion itself, particularly in its relation to art. Whatever the ultimate assumptions and conclusions of her work, Kristeva is not, I think, wrong to add to Aquinas a new emphasis on fantasy, on language, on the body, on mortality, and on the divided, indeed riven, terrain on which we construct and deconstruct ourselves.

What, however, may be said to survive this double critique of religion by psychoanalysis and of theology by *écriture?* There is a point, it seems to me, at which Kristeva meets a limit she cannot quite see over, and, conversely, stops short of the full potential of her own position. The limit has to do first and foremost with the inadequacy of the discourse of art to bear the load she wishes it to bear. Among other things, we can't all, after all, be artists, or writers, or always even very adept or liberating speakers of our own discontents, our desperate and potentially overwhelming ecstasies, our moments of sheer imposition of the *vréel* on the world and on each other. Furthermore, to the extent that we *can* articulate these, we are still dependent on an interlocutor, indeed often on more than one interlocutor, for the effective release and reintegration such articulations can bring. The limits of art and the necessity for community become the more evident the more deeply we explore *écriture.* Kristeva herself recognizes this problem. "But can one," she herself asks, "learn to write? And anyway, who can write alone?"[11]

These questions are partly rhetorical, but they are troubling nonetheless. As Kristeva immediately acknowledges, one "proven balm" for the problems to which they point is religion, which does not require writing and provides, by definition, a certain community.[12] While Kristeva wants, for good reasons, to resist this dangerous *pharmakon,* she no more does so than she begins, inevitably, to articulate a basis for its partial rehabilitation. There is, of course, no formal reason why this option should be foreclosed. As Derrida has remarked about those who discover such potentials in his own thought—those whose work he neither endorses nor condemns — "who could prohibit it? In the name of what?"[13] In fact, there are aspects of Kristeva's work that seem positively to cry out for this supplementation or opening.

We must recognize that in taking up this option we go beyond Kristeva's brief. It is important, however, to choose carefully the openings for doing so in her work. To explore only one such opening, we might mention that Kristeva herself, in her psychoanalytic practice, has come to recognize the necessity for a third, mediating term between the semiotic and the symbolic, between the body of the mother and the law of the father. This term has, I would argue, not only a certain philosophical lineage stemming from Charles Peirce, but a certain religious potential, and a certain bearing on the issue of community as well.[14]

Kristeva associates this third term with Freud's "father of individual prehistory," a shadowy figure outside of the mother-child dyad to whom the mother's desire — Aquinas might say her telos — must, in a healthy situation, be turned.[15] This "father" may or may not, of course, be a literal one. The masculine gender is used only to intensify the point that the mother's eros, her libido, as well as at times, her attention and good will, must be oriented to this other entity. The existence of this third term, or goal, whether figured as father or what Kristeva elsewhere, following Lacan, calls the Great Other, creates the space in the mother-child relationship for individuation and development. It intervenes to allow for that particular mode of psychic energy, so different from, yet so close to, narcissism, hysteria, or regressive identification that she does not hesitate to call *love*.[16]

The necessity Kristeva finds for this concept of the third term — not to mention her use of the word *love*, so clearly borrowed from another rhetoric than that of classical psychoanalysis[17] — opens up a number of possibilities for the return of repressed religion in her work. In order to see these, we must remember that for Kristeva there are occasions on which the analyst must represent or stand in for this third, mediating 'father,' or Great Other.[18] The analyst, however, must not forget the metaphorical nature of this substitution and the relativity of the 'fathering' function to which it refers. If he or she represses or denies this metaphoricity and relativity and pretends to a too literal fulfillment of this role, then the analysand will be subject not to love but to power, to a *Führer*, a tyrant, a psychological dominator, rather than an enabler of cure. In this case, the creative transference that lies at the heart of the therapeutic encounter will fail.[19]

It is possible, however, that the only practice that can keep the analyst (and, ultimately, the analysand) fully aware of this metaphoricity is the recognition of a *Greater* Other, a God the Father in something like a classically religious—I do not say theist or metaphysical—sense of the term. Of course, that greater 'Father' must in no sense be literalized, or rendered monological, or else we should have the same situation of domination in religion both Freud and Kristeva deplore in psychoanalysis. The realization of a relationship to some such posited entity is useful, however, if only as a way of relativizing, for all parties concerned, the overdetermined power of a real father or even a metaphorical father-figure.[20] There is, to put it a little differently, perhaps a way of enunciating that phrase "Our Father" which not only avoids calling down the full force of the patriarchy on the speaker or speakers but also fosters and maintains the health and liberty of the soul.

Needless to say, there are problems with such a strategy of recuperation. Among others, there is the difficulty that the primitive gender marking involved in saying "Our Father," even if understood in this liberating manner, may still prove too threatening to work at its best. As we've said, this masculine gender marking is not gratuitous; it is at least partially motivated, perhaps necessitated, by a need to signify the reorientation of the eros of the mother to another and to prevent a suffocating or devouring passion for the child. Its meaning, however, may be overdetermined, so that it comes down too firmly on the side of the letter of the law. What happens, then, if the addressee of prayer is figured as Son or even Spirit, with the less patriarchal and in some cases more feminine overtones of these terms? The function of these various invocations would depend very much on the particular situation of the individual or community at any given time. (Certainly, there has been more concern in the normative Christian tradition to prevent the regressive potentials of the feminine gender than the equally dangerous abuses of the masculine one.)

To guard against simple reinstatement of the law of the father in its totalizing and death-dealing aspects, however, the "Our Father" or any of its variants must, as has already been fully implied, be invoked in and through a different discourse than that of theology proper, or at least the 'scientific theology' of many current schools of thought. Kristevan *écriture* is certainly one possibility, though it has the limitations mentioned. But perhaps, as my use of the term *invoke* already signals, another, in some ways more adequate, alternative is the discourse of prayer, and more specifically of what I have elsewhere called *prière féminine*, prayer in the feminine mode.[21]

By *prière féminine* I mean, very generally, prayer that is open to everyone, whatever the state of his or her metaphysical convictions or artistic abilities, prayer that does not seek to constitute its object either "outside" or "inside" the self, either as immanent or a transcendent ego ideal, but rather seeks to divest itself of *all* concepts and ideals — even concepts and ideals of Other and/or Self — in order to experience the borderline, the limen, between symbolic and semiotic modes of being. Such prayer seeks not an abstract true-real *(vréel)*, or even an abstract true-real-beautiful *(beau-vréel?)* to which it can cling, but rather looks to find a space for something far more provisional, something "far more deeply interfused." This mode of prayer does not seek to repress the erotic, any more than to exploit it, to empty fantasy, any more than to fulfill it, to negate language any more than to reify or remain bound by it. Nor does it deny death; how could it, when it remains, deliberately, so close to the body and the breath? Because of its explicit acknowledgment of a communal context, moreover, it deliberately opens itself to a collective as well as an individual telos, one that no person and no single petitioner alone can either fully realize or finally delay.

As all the best accounts of such prayer are always concerned to remind us, and as the above very partial and awkward account of it confirms, feminine prayer cannot be spelled out in words, but rather shades off into a silence that is neither the silence of repression nor of a spurious fulsomeness. It can and must, however, as postmodern critics say, be "theorized." We are, after all, talking about a difficult, not an easy, practice, one poised on a knife edge between soma and psyche, quietism and enthusiasm. It requires constant vigilance, vigilance of the kind only rigorous theory and criticism can provide, to keep it from degenerating into regressive bliss or baroque self-inflation.

Kristeva's work is, I think, an important resource for this project. If to make use of this resource we must sometimes read her "outside the camp" — outside, that is, the limits of the (primarily artistic and psychoanalytic) beliefs, practices, and programs she would herself endorse, we must nevertheless do so by working through, not avoiding, the resistances she so clearly articulates. Without the refining fire of psychoanalysis and *écriture*, religion, theology, and even prayer will all too often remain unreconstructed tools of imposition, repression, and terror, leaving no role at all for art, for the body, for the sound of other voices, or for that opening of new psychic and imaginative spaces by which we make room for the numinous in our languages and lives.

## NOTES

1. cf. *In the Beginning Was Love*, trans. Arthur Goldhammer (New York: Columbia University Press, 1987) and a remark cited by Toril Moi, in *The Kristeva Reader*, ed. Toril Moi (New York: Columbia University Press, 1986), "For me, in a

very Christian fashion, ethics merges with love, which is why ethics also merges with the psychoanalytic relationship" 20.

2. "I call 'religion' this phantasmic necessity on the part of speaking beings to provide themselves with a *representation* (animal, female, male, parental, etc.) in place of what constitutes them as such, in other words, symbolization—the double articulation and syntactic sequence of language, as well as its preconditions or substitutes (thoughts, affects, etc.)." (Kristeva, "Women's Time," *The Kristeva Reader* 208)

3. Kristeva elaborates this concept in a technical paper presented to the Service de psychiatrie of the Hospital de la Cité Universitaire that deals with the linguistic manifestations of psychosis (see "The True-Real," *The Kristeva Reader* 216). She situates the split between the order of "truth" and that of "reality" both in terms of the development of Western philosophy and in terms of Freudian theory. The "true-real," or *vréel*, indicates the attempt to collapse these two orders into one another by a kind of willful insistence. It marks both a danger (of fascism and/or psychosis) and "an area of risk and salvation for the speaking being" (217).

4. cf. Kristeva, *Revolution in Poetic Language*, trans. Leon S. Roudiez (New York: Columbia University Press, 1984): "As the place of production for a subject who transgresses the thetic by using it as a necessary boundary—but not as an absolute or as an origin—poetic language and the mimesis from which it is inseparable, are profoundly a-theological. They are not critics of theology but rather the enemy within and without, recognizing both its necessity and its pretensions. In other words, poetic language and mimesis may appear as an argument complicitous with dogma—we are familiar with religion's use of them—but they may also set in motion what dogma represses. In so doing, they no longer act as instinctual floodgates within the enclosure of the sacred and become instead protestors against its posturing. And thus, its complexity unfolded by its practices, the signifying process joins social revolution" (61).

5. Thomas Aquinas, *Summa Theologiae*, part II, q. 84. art. 7. Ed. and trans. Anton C. Pegis, *Introduction to St. Thomas Aquinas* (New York: Modern Library, 1948) 396. My general interpretation of Aquinas is heavily influenced by Pegis, and I am more indebted to his work than a mere footnote can indicate.

6. Kristeva, "Ratio Diligendi, or the Triumph of One's Own, Thomas Aquinas: Natural Love and the Love of Self," in *Tales of Love*, trans. Leon S. Roudiez (New York: Columbia University Press, 1987) 170–89.

7. Umberto Eco, *The Aesthetics of Thomas Aquinas*, trans. Hugh Bredin (Cambridge, Mass: Harvard University Press, 1988). See especially the section "The Beauty of the Son of God," 122–5.

8. Kristeva, *Revolution in Poetic Language*, 23–5.

9. Kristeva, *Powers of Horror: An Essay on Abjection,* trans. Leon S. Roudiez (New York: Columbia University Press, 1982) 120–32. See especially the sections called "Sin as Requisite for the Beautiful," "Avowal: Confession," and "Felix Culpa: Spoken Sin. Duns Scotus," in *Powers of Horror,* 120–32.

10. Kristeva, *Powers of Horror* 115–18; *The Kristeva Reader* 236.

11. Kristeva, "The True-Real," *The Kristeva Reader* 236.

12. Kristeva, "The True-Real," *The Kristeva Reader* 236.

13. Jacques Derrida, "How to Avoid Speaking," *Languages of the Unsayable: The Play of Negativity in Literature and Literary Theory* (New York: Columbia University Press, 1989) 4–70.

14. Kristeva is here influenced by Charles Peirce and American pragmatism, as she herself has acknowledged. The point is further developed in Rebecca Chopp's *The Power to Speak: Feminism, Language, God* (Philadelphia: Crossroads, 1989).

15. Kristeva, *Tales of Love* 33–35.

16. Kristeva, *Tales of Love* 31.

17. The difficult reinstatement of the term *love [amour]* in Kristeva's discourse, a term that gives her almost, though not quite, as much trouble as the term *spirit* does Derrida, is theorized as another term for transference in "Freud and Love: Treatment and Its Discontents," *Tales of Love,* 21–56 and put into literary operation in her preface to that book, "In Praise of Love," 1–17, and in her smaller, carefully wrought *In the Beginning Was Love.*

18. Kristeva takes the term Great Other in part from Lacan. In his "Lacan and the Discourse of Theology," Charles Winquist has warned against a too easy identification of this term with the Judeo-Christian concept of God. He claims that this particular way of theologizing Lacan's Great Other would be a mistake because this concept is construed by Lacan primarily in terms of a lack — the lack of a specific object of desire — and by a function — the function of constituting the human subject. My emphasis on the relativizing function of this Great Other and on its metaphorical dimension is meant to counter precisely what Winquist rightly criticizes as the ultimate identification of that term with a simple theist notion of God. I entirely agree that it would be a mistake to attempt to erect a "positive science of theology" on the basis of this case of mistaken identity; indeed to try to do so would reduce religion to no more than a rationalization of the law of the father, a reduction that, following Kristeva's own theory and practice, I am most concerned to avoid. See Charles E. Winquist, "Lacan and Theological Discourse," *Lacan & Theological Discourse,* ed. Edith Wyschogrod, David Crownfield, and Carl A. Raschke (Albany, New York: State University of New York Press, 1989) 30.

19. Kristeva, *Tales of Love* 31.

20. Both Son and Spirit have been figured in the past, in ways we may not wish to lose sight of today, as feminine or neuter. (See, inter alia, Caroline Walker Bynum, " . . . And Woman His Humanity: Female Imagery in the Religious Writing of the Later Middle Ages," in *Gender and Religion: On the Complexity of Symbols*, ed. Caroline Walker Bynum, Stevan Harrell, and Paula Richman, 257–88.) Indeed the unmarked neuter of the term *spirit* in some languages, English among them, may prove to be even more important as a liberating factor than the explicit feminine marking, which might at times too easily allow a relapse back into the undifferentiated regressions of incest fantasy.

21. In coining the phrase *prière féminine*, I am, of course, thinking of the notion of *écriture féminine* found in some French feminist thought, most notably that of Helene Cixous and Luce Irigaray. I also suspect, though I am not yet able to develop this connection with the care it deserves, that I what I am pointing to here has an affiliation with Edith Wyschogrod's call for what, following Blanchot, she terms a "community of unavowal." Needless to say, these links and affiliations require much more discussion than I can give them here.

## INTER-TEXT 6

Kearns, with Jonte-Pace and Graybeal, has attended primarily to the critical elements of Kristeva's analysis of religion, in contrast to the more affirmative focus in Crownfield. An interesting feature of her treatment is her distinction, more explicit than in Kristeva herself, between religion, which Kristeva subjects to a psychoanalytic critique, and theology, which is given over to a literary—a semiological—analysis.

Kearns understands Kristeva's critique of religion primarily in terms of its fantasy role in masking from us knowledge of our mortality. This assimilates it, for example, to Ernest Becker's thesis, in *The Denial of Death*, that the truth of human mortality is literally unbearable and illusion is necessary to existence. For Becker, we must construct illusions, and the problem is to develop those in which there is the most space for social coexistence and for constructive action. For Kristeva, the emphasis is more pluralistic and more individual: we must learn to play among images, fictions, fantasies of which we are no longer captive. Sociality is important but, as we have seen in the last several articles, it is construed essentially in terms of the establishment and maintenance of a socially functional self or selves. And *jouissance*, enjoyment, ecstasy, including enjoying the play of our own self-division, as Graybeal will remind us, is more central for Kristeva than for Becker.

Kearns notes that religion can also function positively for Kristeva as a "feminine" discourse mediating between the conflictual elements of life (see Jonte-Pace's reservations as well as Graybeal). But this mediating role can be obscured and blocked by the function of theology as rationalization, as logocentric exclusion of difference and division. Kristeva's strategy is to restore an awareness of the character of theology as language, as signifying practice unsettled and relativized by its own archaic semiotic overdetermination. By creating a kind of homology between theological and literary discourse, Kristeva institutes an intertextual displacement by which she intends to liberate the rigorous insightfulness of much theological rhetoric from its dogmatic illusion.

125

It is in support of this agenda that Kearns turns to Thomas Aquinas, the stereotypical logocentric onto-theologian. For Thomas, too, the subject is heterogeneous to itself, as a conjuncture of body and soul; its unity is teleological. But there is also a unifying process in this life, in the operation of the imagination in constructing phantasms by which the universal (which is non-material) can be apprehended in the sensory presence of a corporeal individual. Kearns identifies these phantasms with fantasy, with the sorts of fiction to which Kristeva appeals. The Kristevan fantasy manages the composite of symbolic and semiotic as the Thomistic phantasm does the composite of soul and body.

This must be understood in relation to the Kristevan understanding of language, as entry into public spaces: of the law, of the distinction of self and other, of the shared world of marked differences. For Kristeva, Kearns points out in company with Reineke, Fisher, and others, the symbolic function of language is disrupted by the semiotic rhythms of desire and abjection, the Father's law textured by the maternal *chora* in which it is inscribed. Kearns illustrates this with Kristeva's treatment of sin—at the same time a recognition and a denial of the fundamentally divided and inescapably maternal and semiotic character of the subject.

Religious discourse (and ritual) thus provide sophisticated resources for articulation and management of the sufferings of the divided subject, but at the same time serve to reify, absolutize and thereby conceal and falsify. Kearns introduces in this respect an important notion of Kristeva's not discussed elsewhere in this volume, the *vréel* or "true-real." Kristeva uses this notion to indicate a condition of fusion in which a subject loses the distinction between the signifier and the object, the "true" of discourse and the "real" of our experience of what is heterogeneous to discourse. The subject regards the symbolic representations with the immediacy and insistence appropriate to the things and seems incapable of recognizing that there is a distinction between them. The dogmatic function of theology, which may serve affirmatively to protect a triadic symbolization of the structure of selfhood from collapsing into a dyad (as discussed in Crownfield), may also serve negatively as a law prohibiting recognition of the distinction between signifier and referent in religion, and thus protecting the "true-real" against the pain of partial truth and divided reality.

Art, retaining its awareness of the process of its own construction, recognizing in its plurality and relativity the fissured character of existence, represents an alternative to religion's tendency to freeze its results. The order of knowledge and the order of desire do not, as they do in Aquinas, ultimately meet. But there remains, for Kearns, a limit in

Kristeva's own position that she never comes to recognize. Art is not available to all. Its psychoanalytic analogue depends on an interlocutor. Both assume some sort of community from which the pain of division or the fusion of the true-real may bar us. Collective, imaginary, semiotic, configured around the divine interlocutor, religion bears on this limit — no sooner set aside than it has reemerged, disestablished but still pertinent.

Kearns notes in this context the development in Kristeva's later thought of the figure of the father of individual prehistory (central also to Crownfield's and Reineke's discussions). Not necessarily masculine, this figure is necessarily other to mother. Here Kearns brings in Lacan's notion of the "great Other" ("great" in the sense that it is designated by a capital letter, in distinction from the *"petit autre"* of the object of desire). This is in Lacan the Other of alterity itself, other to discourse and desire as such. Kearns assimilates this notion to the Kristevan idea of mother's other A footnote recognizes Charles Winquist's warning against equation of the Lacanian Other with God, but Kearns's argument may require a stronger affirmative association of the terms than Winquist might accept. (Perhaps Edith Wyschogrod's discussion of Anselm's proof of God's existence in terms of Lacan's Other, found like the Winquist article in *Lacan and Theological Discourse,* provides a middle ground on which Kearns' argument can rest.) At any rate, the Third Party, mother's other, serves as first representative (Kearns at one point says metaphor) of the great Other.

The classical religious (not necessarily metaphysical) figure of God the Father both carries the trace of this originary otherness and serves as outermost representative of the Other, relativizing all [other?] transference objects. In relativizing this figure in turn by psychoanalytic and semiological critique, Kearns (Kristeva) subverts the grip of the true-real. The God-function remains, though, exposed to the ambiguity of the figure of the father, not only the archaic other but the phallic law and thus a petty other of significant negativity. It is the existential exigency for an appeal beyond both phallic law and maternal regression that structures Kearns's notion of *prière féminine,* analogous to contemporary French *écriture féminine* — free, personal, not preoccupied with symbolically constituting its object, not repressing its erotic, its fictional, its mortal character. This is, I think, closely related to the notion of a fictive Christianity at the end of Crownfield's essay; together they suggest that the positive possibilities of religion celebrated also in Graybeal are available in the debris of the Judaic and Christian traditions as well as outside it.

# 7

# JOYING IN THE TRUTH
# OF SELF-DIVISION

### Jean Graybeal

*Jean Graybeal's essay is at the end of this collection because its reflections on self-construction, on* jouissance, *and on* balanse *offer an image of the kind of consequence all the theoretical analysis of the preceding essays might come to life in.*

Julia Kristeva's perspectives on the phenomena of religion defy easy generalization. The wealth of detail in her analyses and their complexity make her works both a joy and a trial to read; they are always provocative and suggestive, never stable or definitive. In this chapter I will first attempt to characterize Kristeva's ideas on religion in a certain way and then suggest a few forms of religious activity that would seem to undermine or serve as counterexamples to her perspective as I have interpreted it.

Kristeva's analysis of religion is profoundly connected to her understanding of the dynamics of the subject; it is the needs and desires of the individual subject that express themselves in religious formations. Kristeva calls her model of the subject *le sujet en procès,* the subject in process or on trial (*procès* carries legal connotations in French). Not an entity of any description, this subject is rather a process suspended over emptiness and balancing between competing yet complementary forces. For Kristeva, the subject is constituted within and through language, which she describes as having two basic dimensions or dispositions between which the subject balances.

Kristeva's work as psychoanalyst has given her insight into these aspects of language, but she sees them at work to some degree in all

129

speaking subjects, not only in those whose discourse displays them most prominently, like her patients, and poets. Kristeva names the two aspects of language the "symbolic" and the "semiotic" and suggests that to fall out of the balance between them and into one or the other exclusively is madness. The "symbolic" side is the aspect of language that makes possible our socially accepted system of meaning. Referential, logical, thetic, it is associated with reason and law, with the social system as it is constituted through common definition.

On the other side of the precarious balance lies the "semiotic" dimension—that which is "heterogeneous" to meaning, truth, logic, and representation. Outside of signification, threatening to meaning, the semiotic dimension signals its presence in discourse through effects of rhythm, nonsense, alliteration, wordplay, repetition, musical effects, laughter, or a dominance of sound over sense.

Kristeva analyzes the dramatic appearance of semiotic effects in the discourse of her patients and in avant-garde literature, places where they are more readily apparent than in ordinary language. But even in everyday speech, both dimensions of language are always present, in some kind of balance. To fall completely into the semiotic side of the balance would mean a full regression to the period of earliest infancy when these patterns of rhythm and wordplay were being acquired, while to fall in the other direction would mean a full immersion in the dominant discourse of the day, avoiding all intrusion from any place that could question or challenge the system of meaning established by the culture.

Identified with the semiotic and symbolic aspects of language in the construction of the subject are a mother and a father. Kristeva argues that in cultures where the primary responsibility for early infant care is assigned primarily to mothers, the semiotic dimension in language is "maternally connoted." The rhythms, echoes, and laughs that cut across the meaning of our language come from our earliest days and are tied up with the primal experience of our mother's body. Our initiation into the rules and laws of language as well as into social conformity is accompanied by the authority of the father, breaking up the idyllic mother-child dyad and thus coming to be associated with the rule-regulated side of language.

The subject thus finds itself in the precarious situation of maintaining a balance between opposing forces, constructing itself as it goes both in relation to what Kristeva (following Lacan) calls the "Name of the Father" (the expression *le nom du père* also suggests the "No of the Father" in French) and to the archaic mother, the imprint of the mother's body that remains associated, in the individual's deep memory, with the rhythms and music of language. According to Kristeva, this description applies equally to the positions of men and of women. Male and female infants follow their own distinctive paths of identification and differentiation, yet each emerges as a subject who is drawn by competing forces. On the one hand, we have separated from the maternal plenum and want at some level to go back there, and on the other hand, we have each both made some kind of peace with the social structure of meaning and law and yet experience alienation within it. Kristeva thus describes the subject as teetering on two brinks at once:

> On the one hand, there is pain — but it also makes one secure — caused as one recognizes oneself as subject of (others') discourse, hence tributary of a universal Law. On the other, there is pleasure — but it kills — at finding oneself different, irreducible, for one is borne by a simply singular speech, not merging with the others, but then exposed to the black thrusts of a desire that borders on idiolect and aphasia.[1]

This "tightrope act" of the subject suspended between semiotic and symbolic does not take place over any sort of safety net that could guarantee the survival of the self in spite of a fall from balance, as though there were an enduring substance or entity at the core of the self; it goes on, rather, over a great emptiness, an emptiness that Kristeva asserts is "at the root of the human psyche."[2] Neither is the balancing act illuminated from above by spotlights. It takes place "beneath the emptiness of heaven."[3]

As I see it, Kristeva's analysis of religion is very largely a phenomenology of one of the subject's two basic categories of options for dealing with its own otherness, dividedness, lack of unity or center. Suspended over an abyss beneath an expanse of emptiness, says Kristeva, the subject has two kinds of possibility open to it. One path is very diverse, containing many sorts of possible means of denying, repressing, or resolving the tensions and anxiety inherent in being a subject in process/on trial. Among these methods are the vast variety of religious formations. The other fundamental possibility for the divided subject is what Kristeva calls *jouissance*. We shall come back to this later; for now let us translate it simply as "joying in the truth of self-division."[4] Rather than attempt to escape or alter the basic condition of division, *jouissance* "joys" in it.

Let us look briefly at some of the characterizations Kristeva assigns to religion. If it makes sense to describe her view of religion as critical or negative, this sense is only relevant in the context of understanding her as psychoanalyst. As analyst, she is not concerned to judge or devalue the neurotic or psychotic strategies of the subject on trial but to understand them. Still, the religious options Kristeva examines seem to be for the most part escapes from the great difficulty of the healthy *jouissance* she would want us all to know.

Consider for a moment her perspective on the options open to feminism today. Kristeva warns feminists against the temptation of turning feminism into a "religion" founded on "its belief in Woman, Her power, Her writing,"[5] and calls for resistance to this temptation. What makes a "religious" solution so generally tempting is the mechanism Kristeva ascribes to it whereby the subject in process/on trial, instead of either stoically tolerating or finding a difficult *jouissance* in its self-division, succeeds in projecting outward its own internal split. Through the processes of sublimation or idealization on the one hand, processes that create a *sacred* image, realm, or idea (such as "Woman" with a capital "W")—and on the other hand, the processes of abjection or perversion, culminating in the projection of a rejected "other," "not I" — the subject seeks to stabilize and secure its identity in relation to these poles of otherness.

Kristeva has called religion the intersection of the paths of sublimation and perversion.[6] These "paths" she seems to see as directions the subject might take to escape from the place where it experiences its self-division. Kristeva's books *Powers of Horror* and *Tales of Love* are erudite and engaging explorations of the evolution of varying versions of this kind of structure. She refers frequently to the violent consequences of this means of denying the emptiness on which we rest, and interprets the complementary motions of sublimation—reaching upward for our anchor in the symbolic realm—and perversion—being drawn all unwilling into what we most vigorously exclude—as foundational to the Western history of repression, persecution, and intolerance. An identity founded on the exclusion of otherness always feels threatened by it . . . and thus feels forced to take measures against it.

"Religion," then, is at least sometimes for Kristeva a code for the denial of difference, both within and without the subject. As such, it comes in for severe criticism, and its end or death becomes an occasion for hope. But can we live without religion in any form? How are we to live without the hope of resolving our split condition, much less "joy" in our self-division? Is it possible?

*Jouissance* is the alternative to which we are called, says Kristeva. Recognizing and in some manner *delighting* in the difference, the otherness, the not-self-ness of self can open up the possibility of "joying in the truth of self-division." *Jouissance* is the subject's double experience of mastery of meaning as well as passage through it. Kristeva puts it this way: "Our only chance to avoid being neither master nor slave of meaning lies in our ability to insure our mastery of it (through technique or knowledge) as well as our passage through it (through play or practice). In a word, *jouissance*."[7]

The subject "masters" the symbolic system — knows what it means, knows how to speak and to participate in the system of which she is a part — and yet is also in touch with the semiotic forces on the other side, which both require and make possible her individual playful passage through that system. Her *jouissance* is her experience of her doubleness, her awareness of the difference within her own identity, of the otherness of her self to her self. "Joying in the truth of self-division" means hearing "in language — and not in the other, nor in the other sex — the gouged-out eye, the wound, the basic incompleteness that conditions the infinite quest of signifying concatenations."[8]

The notion of identity itself is what we must question, says Kristeva. If emptiness is "at the root of the human psyche,"[9] we are called to move toward a practice fully cognizant of the inescapable *nonidentity* of every subject. Such a practice would involve understanding that even the dichotomy "man/woman" belongs to metaphysics[10] and that "sexual identity" or "identity" as a woman or man is finally untenable when the subject itself is seen to be not-one. It means recognizing that the tendency to project difference and otherness outward is at the core of violence and ethical atrocities and therefore means attempting to contain the struggle with otherness in the place where it belongs: within the psyche itself, " . . . in order that the struggle, the implacable difference, the violence be conceived in the very place where it operates with the maximum intransigence, in other words, in personal and sexual identity itself, so as to make it disintegrate in its very nucleus."[11]

Kristeva's program is certainly ambitious; it calls for the "*interiorization of the founding separation of the sociosymbolic contract*, as an introduction of its cutting edge into the very interior of every identity whether subjective, sexual, ideological, or so forth."[12] Classically called the withdrawal of projections, and described in yet another way by Kristeva as recognizing "that you do not take place as such, but as a stance essential to a practice,"[13] this picture of the road to both individual and social health looks truly daunting. Kristeva herself asks the crucial question: "What discourse, if not that of a religion, would be able to support this adventure?"[14] What is Kristeva asking here? Is she saying,

"It surely must *not* be a religion?" Or is she saying, "Whatever it is, it *will* in some sense be a religion?" What could take the place of the sheltering function of religion without simply replicating it? Is it possible to understand ourselves as a "stance," a way of standing, balancing, and moving, rather than as an entity or identity?

Kristeva's interest in literature, especially that of the avant-garde, constitutes part of her own answer to this question. She sees literature and the arts as the arenas within which the tensions, contradictions, and *jouissance* of being subjects-in-process find exploration and expression. Her book *Revolution in Poetic Language* addresses precisely this issue and sees the works of writers like Lautréamont and Mallarmé as controlled experiments in disruption of the symbolic by the semiotic, interrogation of the social realm and subject by that which threatens their unity and rationality. Artistic experimentation is an escape from the impasse between, on the one hand, a stabilized, locked-in, "religious" solution to the dilemma of self-division and, on the other, a fall into madness. Art holds the two sides together in a way that allows *jouissance*, "joying in the truth of self-division."

Kristeva writes about the necessity for art in this somewhat apocalyptic (if not "religious") way:

> What discourse, if not that of a religion, would be able to support this adventure . . . ? The role of what is usually called 'aesthetic practices' must increase . . . in order to emphasize the responsibility which all will immediately face of putting this fluidity into play against the threats of death which are unavoidable whenever an inside and an outside, a self and an other, one group and another, are constituted. At this level of interiorization, what I have called 'aesthetic practices' are undoubtedly nothing other than the modern reply to the eternal question of morality.[15]

Aesthetic practices, she seems to say, prevent the solidification of boundaries, definitions, and identifications, thus requiring the subject to acknowledge the reality of dividedness, along with both the guilt and the *jouissance* which that implies. This perspective is no doubt what leads Kristeva to assert that "the artistic experience . . . appears as the essential component of religiosity," and to say that "it is destined to survive the collapse of historical forms of religion."[16]

But is Kristeva's portrait of religion as a variety of escapes from self-division in some sense a caricature? Does she ignore the side of religion that does allow for and even demand *jouissance*? Her own examples of the *jouissance* to be heard in mystical discourse would seem to furnish a telling counter-example to her own generalizations about religion.

Kristeva often refers to religious discourse, especially that of the mystics, to illustrate her analysis of the speaking subject and its dynamics. She seems intensely interested in religious language and particularly in those aspects of religious discourse where the drive for order, rationality, and security is disrupted by an intense and emotional experience of otherness, groundlessness, or interior difference. Kristeva's readings of writers such as Jeanne Guyon, Bernard de Clairvaux, Eckhart, Spinoza, and even Aquinas, provide a powerful counterpoint to her own primary analysis of religion as prohibitor of *jouissance*[17] and "shelter" for the illusory unitary subject.[18]

To be sure, institutional religion has often experienced the unknowingness of mystical discourse as all too threatening and disruptive and has proceeded accordingly to suppress it; yet this tradition has deep roots in the history of Western religious consciousness. Kristeva's attention to that fact has significantly complicated the task of generalizing about her attitude to religion.

Other counter-examples to the portrait of religion as denial of difference would not be difficult to find. Certainly Buddhist teachings about the illusoriness of self and other and about the essential emptiness or nonidentity of all things, including persons, would be instructive in this context. Does Buddhism not then qualify as a "religion" in Kristeva's sense, or is it her definition of religion itself that comes under question here?

The most intriguing counter-example I have met with recently was described in an article by Karen McCarthy Brown entitled "Women's Leadership in Haitian Vodou."[19] Brown's analysis of the healing efficacy of Vodou rituals centers on Vodou's basic understanding and evaluation of conflict. Conflict is accepted and even valued in Vodou, according to Brown, "*as an inevitable, in fact essential, ingredient of life.*"[20] The existence of conflict, or the experience of conflict, is thus not what the Vodou ritual aims to heal. Rather than ridding the self or the social situation of conflict, rather than seeking a tranquilized position or a resolution of conflict, the function of ritual is to allow the subject to develop a way to *balanser,* a way to move or dance within and among the various forces present in the situation.[21]

Brown likens this *balanse* to the active role of the listener or dancer in polyrhythmic African drumming. Drawing on a study of the structure of African drumming,[22] Brown compares the balancing dance of the individual among the various strong forces pulling in different directions to the "metronome sense" or "way of being steady within a context of multiple rhythms" of the one who actively hears, understands, and moves to polyrhythmic African drumming.[23] Drawn by opposing forces from both within and without the self, a strong and healthy person, from the point of view of Vodou, is one who can be "steady within a context of multiple rhythms," moving, spinning, responsive both to the multiple spirits within and to the exigencies of external relationships, but always with a fluid yet strong sense of self. Thus to find or create one's own sense of rhythm, one's own "metronome sense," which can both synchronize with and yet differ from the rhythms of those "others" both within and without, is the religious aim of Vodou.

To my ears this description of Vodou religion sounds very much like the open, fluid sense of self Kristeva advocates and that she ordinarily counterposes to "religion." Not tranquilized, neither projecting into some ideal realm the possibility of resolution and peace nor abjecting onto an enemy the source of conflict, but moving, staying steady, and balancing, the Vodou practitioner as Brown describes her is a virtual model of Kristeva's *jouissance*, "joying in the truth of self-division." We might even want to see her as balancing between the symbolic dimension of identity, meaning, and mastery and the semiotic dimension of nonsense, multiplicity, and laughter. Brown writes about the laughter evoked by one of the Vodou spirits when he is in possession of the Vodou priestess: "To laugh is to balance, and like all balancing within Vodou, is achieved not through resolving or denying conflict, but by finding a way of staying steady in the midst of it."[24]

I would be reluctant to deny the "religious" character of the Vodou worldview and ritual. Perhaps what is needed is to recognize that there are indeed profound religious traditions (like mysticism, like Buddhism, like Vodou) that emphasize precisely the importance of knowing "that you do not take place as such, but as a stance essential to a practice,"[25] as a balance essential to a dance, as a suspension over emptiness essential to *jouissance*.

Kristeva's interest in mystical discourse shows that her perspective on religion is not univocal. She knows that religion is not fully reducible to its sheltering, tranquilizing function, although she does seem to emphasize this dimension. I have attempted to argue here that there may be many examples of religious practices that promote, instead of tranquilization, a very "Kristevan" unease, an unresolved negotiation of ambiguity and nonidentity. The variegated phenomena of religions present even scholars with opportunities of our own for *jouissance*, as we attempt to remain resolutely within their polyrhythmic complexity and to allow them to challenge our own capacities for joying in the truth of self-division.

## NOTES

1. Julia Kristeva, *Desire in Language: A Semiotic Approach to Literature and Art*, ed. Leon S. Roudiez (New York: Columbia University Press, 1980) x.

2. Julia Kristeva, *Tales of Love*, trans. Leon S. Roudiez (New York: Columbia University Press, 1987) 23.

3. Kristeva, *Desire in Language* xi.

4. Julia Kristeva, *Powers of Horror: An Essay on Abjection*, trans. Leon S. Roudiez (New York: Columbia University Press, 1982) 89.

5. Julia Kristeva, "Women's Time," trans. Alice Jardine and Harry Blake, *Signs* 7, no. 1 (Autumn 1981) 33.

6. Kristeva, *Powers of Horror* 89.

7. Kristeva, *Desire in Language* x.

8. Kristeva, *Powers of Horror* 88–89.

9. Kristeva, *Tales of Love* 23.

10. Kristeva, *Tales of Love* 23.

11. Kristeva, "Women's Time" 34.

12. Kristeva, "Women's Time" 35 (emphasis in the original).

13. Kristeva, "Novel as Polylogue," *Desire in Language* 165.

14. Kristeva, "Women's Time" 34.

15. Kristeva, "Women's Time" 35.

16. Kristeva, *Powers of Horror* 17.

17. Julia Kristeva, *Revolution in Poetic Language*, trans. Leon Roudiez (New York: Columbia University Press, 1984) 80.

18. Kristeva, *Revolution in Poetic Language* 70.

19. Karen McCarthy Brown, "Women's Leadership in Haitian Vodou,"

*Weaving the Visions,* ed. Judith Plaskow and Carol Christ (New York: Harper and Row, 1989) 226–34.

20. Brown, "Women's Leadership in Haitian Vodou" 226 (emphasis in original).

21. "In the Vodou context, the Creole word *balanse* refers, among other things, to a kind of ritual movement or dance." Brown, "Women's Leadership in Haitian Vodou" 232.

22. John Miller Chernoff, *African Rhythm and African Sensibility: Aesthetics and Social Action in African Musical Idiom* (Chicago: University of Chicago Press, 1979). Cited by Brown, 228–34 passim.

23. Brown, "Women's Leadership in Haitian Vodou" 229, 233.

24. Brown, "Women's Leadership in Haitian Vodou" 233.

25. Kristeva, "Novel as Polylogue," *Desire in Language* 165.

## INTER-TEXT 7

The theme of the division of the self has been developed in various respects by all our authors; Graybeal brings it back out of the various technical contexts to focus on its human significance: the problem of being always in process and on trial, divided between the social law of the symbolic and the heterogeneity of the semiotic, and the need for self-construction that achieves some sort of balance or coexistence between the two. The options for such balance are either on the side of denial or on that of *jouissance*, which I have elsewhere rendered "ecstatic enjoyment," but which Graybeal, quoting Kristeva, gives as "joying in the truth of self-division." While she cites Kristeva's phrase, "the subject *en procès*" (in process, and on trial), she really develops, with a good basis in the texts, the image of the possibility of a subject *at play* in the differences. (This is still a subject playing like a child on a cliff, constantly in danger yet joying even in the danger itself.)

It is this emphasis on enjoyment of the division itself that distinguishes Graybeal's essay. She attends to the theme of religion in Kristeva primarily from the perspective of its functions as illusion and denial; but like Jonte-Pace and Kearns, who also focus on this aspect, she sees in Kristeva's work itself the marks of a more positive possibility. Through knowledge and technique we acquire some mastery of the symbolic and awareness of its limits, and through play and practice (see Fisher on practice and also Kearns on prayer) we live and move through it. Crucial to this is the acceptance of emptiness and nonidentity. One major option for symbolic support for such acceptance, such practice, is religion.

Graybeal underscores the ambiguance of the theme of religion in Kristeva's essays of the 1970s, on which she focuses. Like Kristeva herself in her later work, Graybeal sees intertwined with the negativities of religion these positive resources for the support of *jouissance*. While Reineke's appropriation of Kristeva for religious studies centers on abjection and sacrifice, Graybeal looks directly for religious support for process, emptiness, division, and enjoyment. Unlike Crownfield and

Kearns, who look primarily to Judaic and Christian materials, she attends to other traditions, and especially to Haitian Vodou.

The central image she develops is that of *balanse*. The image of dancing to multiple rhythms evokes the moving subject in the midst of conflicting forces, steadied by a self-centering "metronome sense" that can play in laughter and nonsense in the midst of the law of the symbolic and the beat of the semiotic. Vodou thus becomes an introductory example of how a Kristevan hermeneutics of recovery could be utilized in the study of various religions, while at the same time its theme of *balanse* becomes an image of the divided self, between the rhythms of the archaic *chora* and those of the law, without solidity or place, moving and playing and joying in self-division.

# EXTRA-TEXT: QUESTIONS

Rather than a conclusion, I want to identify at this end of the book some of the major unfinished questions around which the discussion will go on.

Diane Jonte-Pace has proposed that the common homology of woman and religion reflects a function of woman as metaphor/screen for difference, ultimately for death. In response, I have noted that for Kristeva a subject is constructed as a screen over emptiness, in primordial differentiation out of the maternal *chora*. This suggests that the fearful and abhorrent is at bottom the nothingness of self; metonymically, mother would then be the most immediate representative of that nothingness; fear of death, too, would be its metaphor rather than its original. In support of Jonte-Pace's desire to disassociate woman and death, it might in the light of these issues be necessary to deconstruct self (and woman and death) more radically than has yet been attempted.

Marilyn Edelstein includes in her essay some consideration of whether the identification of self as mother is implied in "Stabat Mater," whether this is readable by one who does not function as mother, whether it is an appropriate or necessary aspect of the question of woman self. This is, I think, a part of the whole problematic of difference: can I understand one who is different from me? Can my identity be informed by, modeled in relation to, the life of another whose experience is incompatible with my difference, my gender, my anatomy, my sexuality, my politics? Edelstein and Kristeva agree that approaches which must exclude difference are narcissistic and undesirable. In view of the diversity of feminist criticisms of Kristeva, it seems appropriate to raise the question (implicit in Edelstein) of what understandings of narcissism those critics would offer—of how they would differ from the substance of Kristeva's analysis, and not simply from the politics or the identity-images they find in her conclusions.

The question of deconstructive exposure of the emptiness of self and the question of transcendental collapse of discourse pose real problems for Crownfield's interest in retrieving a deconstructed Chris-

141

tianity. Kristeva suggests at the end of *Tales of Love* and, less sharply, at the end of *In the Beginning Was Love,* that the collapse of the self-space formerly held open by the triadic character of Christian discourse may not call for some sort of reconstruction of that space, but rather for doing without self-space. Is this possible? Can we play with the emptiness, with the memory of the maternal, with the murderous undertow of language and law, inventing and subverting subjects, roles, stories, images that are lucid about coming from nowhere — without nihilism? Kristeva's images here may be themselves traces of illusion, of a postmodern form of Freud's fantasy of a scientific discourse that could unmask illusion—a fiction of a non-subject that is free of illusion about not being free of illusion. Or Crownfield may be clinging to the semiotics of infancy in looking for further uses for those old stories. Or both.

Martha Reineke makes clear that Kristeva's account of narcissism and self-formation bears heavily on the problems of gender and of the abjection of women. But it is not so clear exactly what that bearing is. The archaic father is not the phallic father; archaic mother is not the identity-model of the feminine. The others of individual prehistory are gendered only in retrospect. Does Reineke assume a definition of gender through identification with parental prototypes and then read it back into prehistory? Are we not all constituted in both identification and rage with both archaic mother and mother's archaic other? How, then, does Kristeva's account succeed in bringing the question of gender into relation to the archaic emergence of self? Is it that Kristeva herself is not clear here? Perhaps that would be one reason her critics are so disturbed by her discussion of the maternal and the pregenital. Does it resolve, or clarify, the problem to see the identification of gender with the archaic parent as metaphor, as an inscribing of the semiotic in the symbolic order?

David Fisher would develop an ethics as signifying practice, negativizing narcissism in inscribing a subject in the public world, both by discourse and practice, in a relational way. Kristeva's later work is illuminated by this conception, in that her analyses of abjection, of love, of faith, of melancholy, and of the stranger all function to examine public inscriptions of subject or self and their relations to the problem of narcissism. (There is not much direct attention in the later texts to practice as material engagement in the different and resistant, but the textual practices she examines clearly have import beyond utterance itself.) What is the interplay between the fictive plurality of discourse and the resistant persistence of the others? Itself plural, partial, only fictively expressible, does otherness not also demand a constancy of address, of

recognition of claim and need and refusal, a community of moral signification? Can we preserve both the fictive plurality of self-being and
the social constancy of the claim of the other? Can there be a discursive
constancy in the ways in which the Symbolic acknowledges the Real
without lapsing into reification and dogma, into false selves and phallic
mastery?

For Cleo Kearns, just as imagination makes perceptual realism
possible in Aquinas, so imagination can enable our postmodern relation to the Great Other, to alterity itself. Without the wishful blindness
of self-deceptive religion, or the dogmatic reification and exclusiveness
of traditional theology, it becomes possible to construct and deconstruct
a transference relation to Other. Indeed, she suggests that transference
to an analyst is a sort of idolatry until its metaphorical marking of the
Really Other becomes clear. A (deconstructed) classical doctrine of God
the Father marks the fundamental transference through which the vi-
cissitudes of life can be engaged and ordinary illusions relativized. De-
patriarchalized in a feminine prayer, such a figure can still enable our
ongoing. Again, is it possible to deconstruct this sort of transference as
thoroughly as the classic psychoanalytic myth supposes the psychoanalytic transference is resolved? Has Kristeva, in pluralizing our fictive
articulations of self and life-space, merely hidden a transferential illusion (or a transcendental necessity for transference??) behind the multiplicity? Or is Kearns constructing a fictional unity by a Thomistic strategy and around a Thomistic teleology?

Jean Graybeal, in her central use of the images of balance and of
dance, gives the discussion a somatic concreteness that talk of discourse and fiction tends to neglect. It is particularly powerful because
both dance and balance in general involve law, regularity, control. The
rhythms of both the symbolic and the semiotic are incarnate in movement; both balancing on the brink(s) and polyrhythmic dancing require
at once strict compliance with the law and full enactment of the semiotics of the flesh. Texts, and speech, Kristeva would have us notice, are
always doing both things at once; her theory of poetic language is an
account of the fleshly dance and balance that animate language in the
work and play of poetry and fiction. Self is, for Graybeal, this activity of
dancing and balancing in its concurrent responsiveness to the archaic
rhythms of the body and the formal metrics of the Law of the Father. But
to a spectator, a dancer's movement looks easy. When the rhythms in
play include the violence of birth and separation, the emptiness of self
and of death, the negativity of law and the sacrificial foundations of the
social, is it possible to dance? Above all it is possible to dance and also

to know the emptiness and negativity, or are we like the cartoon character that keeps running even over the abyss, but plunges as soon as he notices there is no ground under him?

Kristeva's texts, and these discussions of them, suggest that we live in these questions, and deal with them in a diversity of practices all of which involve fiction, illusion, failure, yet all of which involve existing, ongoing, for the time being. Is that enough?

# SELECTED BIBLIOGRAPHY

Note: Most of the bibliography has been compiled by Diane Jonte-Pace and Marilyn Edelstein. All works cited in this volume are included, but it is not a comprehensive listing of works by or about Julia Kristeva.

Ashbery, John. *A Wave: Poems*. New York: Viking Press, 1981.

Bakhtin, Mikhail. *The Dialogic Imagination: Four Essays of M. M. Bakhtin*. Trans. Caryl Emerson and Michael Holquist; ed. Michael Holquist. Austin: University of Texas Press, 1981.

———. "From Notes Made in 1970–71." In *Speech Genres and Other Late Essays*, trans. Vern W. McGee; eds. Caryl Emerson and Michael Holquist. Austin, University of Texas Press, 1986.

Bernstein, Richard. *Praxis and Action*. Philadelphia: University of Pennsylvania Press, 1971.

Beauvoir, Simone de. *The Second Sex*. Trans. Howard M. Parshley. New York: Random House, 1952 (1949).

Becker, Ernest. *The Denial of Death*. New York: The Free Press, 1973.

Bell, Rudolph M. *Holy Anorexia*. Chicago: University of Chicago Press, 1985.

Brown, Karen McCarthy, "Women's Leadership in Haitian Vodou." In *Weaving the Visions*, eds. Judith Plaskow and Carol Christ, 226–234. New York: Harper and Row, 1989.

"Bulgaria." In *New Catholic Encyclopedia*, ed. Catholic University of America. Vol. II. New York: Routledge, 1990.

Butler, Judith. *Gender Trouble: Feminism and the Subversion of Identity*. New York: Routledge, 1990.

———. "Gender Trouble: Feminist Theory and Psychoanalytic Discourse." In *Feminism/Postmodernism*, ed. Linda J. Nicholson, 324–340. New York: Routledge, 1990.

Bynum, Carolyn Walker. " . . . And Woman His Humanity: Female Imagery in the Religious Writing of the Later Middle Ages." In *Gender and Religion: On the Complexity of Symbols*, eds. Carolyn Walker Bynum, Stevan Harrell, and Paula Richman, 257–288. Boston: Beacon Press, 1986.

Chambers, Ross. *Story and Situation: Narrative Seduction and the Power of Fiction*. Minneapolis: University of Minnesota Press, 1984.

Chernoff, John Miller. *African Rhythm and African Sensibility: Aesthetics and Social Action in African Musical Idiom*. Chicago: University of Chicago Press, 1979.

Chodorow, Nancy. *The Reproduction of Mothering: Psychoanalysis and the Sociology of Gender.* Berkeley: University of California Press, 1978.

Chopp, Rebecca. *The Power to Speak: Feminism, Language, God*. Philadelphia: Crossroads, 1989.

Clark, Katerina, and Michael Holquist. *Mikhail Bakhtin*. Cambridge, Mass.: Belknap-Harvard University Press, 1984.

Clark, Suzanne. "Julia Kristeva and the Feminine Subject." Division on Language Theory, MLA Convention. Washington, D.C., 29 Dec. 1989.

Cornell, Drucilla, and Adam Thurschwell. "Feminism, Negativity, Intersubjectivity." In *Feminism as Critique: On the Politics of Gender,* eds. Seyla Benhabib and Drucilla Cornell, 143–162. Minneapolis: University of Minnesota Press, 1987.

Crampton, R. J. *A Short History of Modern Bulgaria*. Cambridge: Cambridge University Press, 1987.

de Man, Paul. "Dialogue and Dialogism." *Poetics Today* 4 (1983). Also in *Rethinking Bakhtin: Extensions and Challenges*, eds. Gary Saul Morson and Caryl Emerson, 105–114. Evanston: Northwestern University Press, 1989.

Derrida, Jacques. "How to Avoid Speaking." In *Languages of the Unsayable: The Play of Negativity in Literature and Literary Theory,* eds. Stanford Budick and Wolfgang Iser, 4–70. New York: Columbia University Press, 1989.

———. "White Mythology: Metaphor in the Text of Philosophy." In *Margins of Philosophy,* trans. Alan Bass, 207–271. Chicago, University of Chicago Press, 1982.

DuBois, Page. *Sowing the Body: Psychoanalysis and Ancient Representations of Women*. Chicago: University of Chicago Press, 1988.

Eco, Umberto, *The Aesthetics of Thomas Aquinas*. Trans. Hugh Bredin. Cambridge, Mass.: Harvard University Press, 1988.

Engelsman, Joan Chamberlain. *The Feminine Dimension of the Divine*. Philadelphia: Westminster Press, 1979.

Foucault, Michel. "The Subject and Power." Afterword. *Michel Foucault: Beyond Structuralism and Hermeneutics.* Eds. Hubert L. Dreyfus and Paul Rabinow, 208–226. Chicago: University of Chicago Press, 1982.

Freud, Sigmund. *The Standard Edition of the Complete Psychological Works of Sigmund Freud* (SE). Trans. J. Strachey. 24 volumes. London: Hogarth Press (New York: W. W. Norton), 1953–1964.

———. *Beyond the Pleasure Principle.* London: Hogarth Press, 1955 (SE 18).

———. "Female Sexuality." New York: W. W. Norton, 1961 (SE 21).

———. *The Future of an Illusion.* New York: W. W. Norton, 1961 (SE 21).

———. *Leonardo Da Vinci and a Memory of His Childhood.* New York: W. W. Norton, 1964 (SE 11).

———. "Obsessive Actions and Religious Practices." London: Hogarth, 1961 (SE 9).

———. "Some Psychical Consequences of the Anatomical Distinction Between the Sexes." New York: W. W. Norton, 1961 (SE 19).

———. "Subtleties of a Parapraxis." In *Character and Culture.* New York: Macmillan, 1963 (SE 16).

———. "The Theme of the Three Caskets." In *Character and Culture.* New York: Macmillan, 1963 (SE 12).

———. *Three Essays on the Theory of Sexuality.* New York: W. W. Norton, 1961 (SE 7).

———. *Totem and Taboo.* New York: W. W. Norton, 1961 (SE 13).

Frosh, Steven. *The Politics of Psychoanalysis: An Introduction to Freudian and Post-Freudian Theory.* New Haven: Yale University Press, 1987.

Gallop, Jane. *The Daughter's Seduction: Feminism and Psychoanalysis.* Ithaca: Cornell University Press, 1982.

———. *Reading Lacan.* Ithaca: Cornell University Press, 1985.

Girard, René. "Discussion." *Violent Origins: Walter Burkert, René Girard, and Jonathan Z. Smith on Ritual Killing and Cultural Formation,* ed. Robert G. Hamerton-Kelly. Stanford: Stanford University Press, 1987.

———. *Violence and the Sacred.* Trans. Patrick Gregory. Baltimore: The Johns Hopkins University Press, 1977.

Grosz, Elizabeth. *Sexual Subversions: Three French Feminists.* Sydney: Allen and Unwin, 1989.

Hamilton, Victoria. *Narcissus and Oedipus: The Children of Psychoanalysis*. London: Routledge & Kegan Paul, 1982.

Irigaray, Luce. "Women, the sacred and money." *Paragraph* 8 (1986): 6–18.

Jardine, Alice. "Gynesis." In *Critical Theory Since 1965*, eds. Hazard Adams and Leroy Searle, 560–570. Tallahassee: Florida State University Press, 1986.

———. *Gynesis: Configurations of Woman and Modernity*. Ithaca: Cornell University Press, 1985.

———. "Opaque Texts and Transparent Contexts: The Political Difference of Julia Kristeva." In Miller, *The Poetics of Gender*. 96–116.

Johnson, Barbara. Translator's Introduction. *Dissemination*. By Jacques Derrida. Trans. Barbara Johnson, vii–xxxiii. Chicago: University of Chicago Press, 1981.

Jones, Ann Rosalind. "Julia Kristeva on Femininity: The Limits of a Semiotic Politics." *Feminist Review* 18 (1984): 56–73.

Jonte-Pace, Diane. "Object Relations Theory, Mothering, and Religion: Toward a Feminist Psychology of Religion." *Horizons* 14, 2, 1987.

———. "Religion: A Rorschachian Projection Theory." *American Imago* 42, 2, 1985.

Kofman, Sara. *The Enigma of Woman: Woman in Freud's Writings*. Trans. Catherine Porter. Ithaca: Cornell University Press, 1985.

Kristeva, Julia. *Black Sun: Depression and Melancholia*. Trans. Leon S. Roudiez. New York: Columbia University Press, 1989.

———. *Desire in Language: A Semiotic Approach to Literature and Art*. Trans. Leon S. Roudiez. New York: Columbia University Press, 1980 (1977).

———. *Étrangers à nous-mêmes*. Paris: Fayard, 1988.

———. *In The Beginning Was Love: Psychoanalysis and Faith*. Trans. Arthur Goldhammer. New York: Columbia University Press, 1987 (1985).

———. "An Interview With Julia Kristeva." With Edith Kurzweil. *Partisan Review* 53 (1986): 216–229.

———. *The Kristeva Reader*. Ed. Toril Moi. New York, Columbia University Press, 1986.

———. "Motherhood According to Giovanni Bellini." In *Desire in Language*. 237–270.

———. "My Memory's Hyperbole." Trans. Athena Viscusi. In *The Female Autograph*, ed. Domna C. Stanton. Spec. issue of *New York Literary Forum* 12–13 (1984): 261–276.

———. "A New Type of Intellectual: The Dissident." Trans. Seán Hand, 292–300. *The Kristeva Reader.*

———. "The Novel as Polylogue." *Desire in Language.* 159–209.

———. "Oscillation between power and denial." [Interview] With Xavière Gauthier. Trans. Marilyn A. August, 165–167. In Marks, *New French Feminisms: An Anthology.*

———. "Postmodernism?" *Romanticism, Modernism, Postmodernism.* Ed. Harry R. Garvin. Spec. issue of *Bucknell Review* 25 (1980): 136–141.

———. *Powers of Horror: An Essay on Abjection.* Trans. Leon S. Roudiez. New York: Columbia University Press, 1982 (1980).

———. *Revolution in Poetic Language.* Trans. Margaret Waller. New York: Columbia University Press, 1984.

———. "Stabat Mater." *Histoires d'amour.* Paris; Denoël, 1983. 225–247.

———. "Stabat Mater." Trans. Leon S. Roudiez, 160–186. In *The Kristeva Reader.*

———. *Strangers to Ourselves.* Trans. Leon S. Roudiez. New York: Columbia University Press, 1991.

———. "The System and the Speaking Subject." Trans. Toril Moi, 24–33. *The Kristeva Reader.*

———. *Tales of Love.* Trans. Leon S. Roudiez. New York: Columbia University Press, 1987 (1983).

———. "Two Interviews With Julia Kristeva." With Elaine Hoffman Baruch and Perry Meisel. *Partisan Review* 51, 2 (1985): 120–132.

———. "Woman Can Never Be Defined." [Interview] Trans. Marilyn A. August, 137–141. In Marks, *New French Feminisms.*

———. "Women's Time." Trans. Alice Jardine and Harry Blake. In *The Kristeva Reader,* 188–213.

———. "Word, Dialogue, and Novel." *Desire in Language.* 64–91.

Lacan, Jacques, *Écrits: A Selection.* Trans. Alan Sheridan. New York: W. W. Norton, 1977 (1966).

———. *Four Fundamental Concepts of Psychoanalysis.* Trans. Alan Sheridan. New York: Norton, 1981 (1973).

———. *Feminine Sexuality: Jacques Lacan and the École Freudienne.* Ed. Jacqueline Rose and Juliet Mitchell. New York: Norton, 1982.

———. "God and the Jouissance of the Woman" and "A Love Letter." Trans. Jacqueline Rose, 137–161. *Feminine Sexuality: Jacques Lacan and the École Freudienne.*

———. "The Signification of the Phallus." In *Écrits: A Selection*. 281–291.

———. "The Subversion of the Subject and the Dialectic of Desire in the Freudian Unconscious." In *Écrits: A Selection*. 291–325.

Laplanche, Jacques. *Life and Death in Psychoanalysis*. Trans. J. Mehlman. Baltimore: Johns Hopkins University Press, 1976 (1970).

Lechte, John. *Julia Kristeva*. New York: Routledge, 1990.

MacIntyre, Alasdair. *After Virtue*. 2d Ed. Notre Dame: University of Notre Dame Press, 1984.

Marks, Elaine, and Isabelle de Courtivron, eds. *New French Feminisms: An Anthology*. New York: Schocken Books, 1981.

Merleau-Ponty, Maurice. *The Visible and the Invisible*. Trans. Alphonso Lingis. Evanston: Northwestern University Press, 1966.

Miller, Nancy K., ed. *The Poetics of Gender*. New York: Columbia University Press, 1986.

Mitchell, Juliet. "Introduction I." In Lacan, *Feminine Sexuality: Jacques Lacan and the École Freudienne*, 1–26.

———. *Psychoanalysis and Feminism*. New York: Pantheon Books, 1974.

———. *Women: The Longest Revolution*. New York: Random House, 1984.

Moi, Toril. *Sexual/Textual Politics: Feminist Literary Theory*. London and New York: Methuen, 1985.

Nietzsche, Friedrich. "On Truth and Lying in an Extra-Moral Sense." 1873. *Friedrich Nietzsche on Rhetoric and Language*. Trans. and ed. Sander L. Gilman, Carole Blair, and David J. Parent, 246–257. New York: Oxford University Press, 1989.

———. *The Will to Power*. Vol. II. Trans. Anthony M. Ludovici. New York: Russell and Russell, 1964.

Ong, Walter J., S. J. "The Writer's Audience is Always a Fiction." *PMLA* 90 (1975): 9–21.

Rabinowitz, Peter. "Truth in Fiction: A Reexamination of Audiences." *Critical Inquiry* 4 (1977): 121–141.

Ragland-Sullivan, Ellie. *Jacques Lacan and the Philosophy of Psychoanalysis*. Chicago: University of Illinois, 1987.

Rawls, John. *A Theory of Justice*. Cambridge, Mass.: Harvard University Press, 1971.

Readings, Bill, "The Deconstruction of Politics." In *Reading De Man Reading*, eds. Lindsay Walters and Wlad Godzich, 223–243. Minneapolis: University of Minnesota Press, 1989.

Reineke, Martha. " 'The Devils Are Come Down Upon Us': Myth, History, and the Witch as Scapegoat." *Union Seminary Quarterly Review*. Spring, 1990, 55 –83.

———. "Life Sentences: Kristeva and the Limits of Modernity." *Soundings* 71 (1988): 439–461.

———. " 'This Is My Body': Reflections on Abjection, Anorexia, and Medieval Women Mystics." *Journal of the American Academy of Religion* 58, 2 (1990) 245–265.

Ricoeur, Paul. *The Rule of Metaphor*. Trans. Robert Czerny with Kathleen McLaughlin and John Costello, S. J. Toronto: University of Toronto Press, 1977.

Rieff, Philip. *Freud: The Mind of the Moralist*. Chicago: University of Chicago Press, 1979.

Rizzuto, Anne. *The Birth of the Living God: A Psychoanalytic Study*. Chicago: University of Chicago Press, 1979.

Rose, Jacqueline. "Introduction II." In Lacan, *Feminine Sexuality: Jacques Lacan and the École Freudienne*. 27–57.

———. "Julia Kristeva — Take Two." *Sexuality in the Field of Vision*. London: Verso, 1986. 141–164.

Rubin, Gayle. "The Traffic in Women: Notes on the 'Political Economy' of Sex." In *Toward an Anthropology of Women*, ed. R. Reiter, 157–210. New York: Monthly Review Press, 1975.

Ruether, Rosemary. "Misogyny and Virginal Feminism in the Fathers of the Church." In *Religion and Sexism*, ed. R. Ruether New York: Simon and Schuster, 1974.

Schrag, Calvin. *Communicative Praxis and the Space of Subjectivity*. Bloomington: Indiana University Press, 1986.

Schurmann, Reiner. *Heidegger on Being and Acting: From Principles to Anarchy*. Trans. Christine-Marie Gros. Bloomington: Indiana University Press, 1987.

Smith, Paul. *Discerning the Subject*. Minneapolis: University of Minnesota Press, 1988.

———. "Julia Kristeva Et Al.; or, Take Three or More." In *Feminism and Psycho-*

*analysis,* ed. Richard Feldstein and Judith Roof, 84–104. Ithaca: Cornell University Press, 1989.

Stanton, Domna C. "Difference on Trial: A Critique of the Maternal Metaphor in Cixous, Irigaray, and Kristeva." In Miller, *The Poetics of Gender,* 157–182.

Stepelevich, Lawrence S., and David Lamb, eds. *Hegel's Philosophy of Action.* Atlantic Highlands: Humanities Press, 1983.

Stevens, Wallace. *The Collected Poems of Wallace Stevens.* New York: Alfred A. Knopf, 1977.

Taylor, Mark. *Altarity.* Chicago: University of Chicago Press, 1987.

———. "Refusal of the Bar." In Wyschogrod, *Lacan and Theological Discourse,* 39–53.

Thomas Aquinas. *Introduction to St. Thomas Aquinas.* Ed. and trans. Anton C. Pegis. New York: Modern Library, 1948.

Todorov, Tzvetan. *Mikhail Bakhtin.* Trans. Wlad Godzich. Minneapolis: University of Minnesota Press, 1984.

Van Herik, Judith. *Freud on Femininity and Faith.* Berkeley: University of California Press, 1982.

Walzer, Michael. *Spheres of Justice: A Defense of Pluralism and Equality.* New York: Basic Books, 1983.

Winnicott, D. W. *Playing and Reality.* New York: International Universities Press, 1971.

———. "Transitional Objects and Transitional Phenomena." *International Journal of Psychoanalysis* 34 (1953): 89–97.

Winquist, Charles. "Lacan and Theological Discourse." In Wyschogrod, *Lacan and Theological Discourse,* 26–38.

Wyschogrod, Edith, David Crownfield, and Carl Raschke, eds. *Lacan and Theological Discourse.* Albany: State University of New York Press, 1989.

# CONTRIBUTORS

**David Crownfield** is professor of religion and philosophy at the University of Northern Iowa. He holds a Th.D. in systematic theology from Harvard and is co-editor of *Lacan and Theological Discourse*.

**Marilyn Edelstein** is assistant professor of English at Santa Clara University. She holds a Ph.D. in English from the State University of New York at Buffalo.

**David Fisher** is associate professor of philosophy at North Central College. He holds a Ph.D. in theology from Vanderbilt University.

**Jean Graybeal** is associate professor of religion and chair of the Department of Religious Studies at California State University at Chico and is author of *Language and "The Feminine" in Nietzsche and Heidegger*. She holds a Ph.D. in religion from Syracuse University.

**Diane Jonte-Pace** is assistant professor of religion at Santa Clara University. She holds a Ph.D. in the psychology of religion from the University of Chicago.

**Cleo Kearns** is visiting scholar at Princeton Theological Seminary. She holds a Ph.D. in comparative literature from Columbia University.

**Martha Reineke** is assistant professor of religion and director of Women's Studies at the University of Northern Iowa. She holds a Ph.D. in theology from Vanderbilt University.

153

# INDEX

abject, abjection, xvi, xix, 10, 24, 25, 42, 49, 51, 58, 60, 61, 75–82, 87, 92, 94, 98–101

absence, 2, 12–25, 34, 42, 75, 98

aesthetics. *See* art

alterity, 6, 13, 14, 18, 19, 32, 53, 127, 143

apocalypse, 80, 88

Aquinas. *See* Thomas Aquinas

archaic (*See also* prehistory), xvi, xviii, 10, 18, 19, 25, 41, 44, 54, 59, 60, 65, 66, 73, 75–82, 87, 88, 92–94, 98–100, 102, 108, 125, 127, 130, 140, 142, 143

Aristotle, 94, 104

art, xix, 9, 20, 37, 44–47, 52, 96, 111–114, 116, 117, 120, 121, 126, 127, 134

Ashbery, John, 106

Augustine, 8, 11

Bakhtin, Mikhail, x–xii, 31, 32, 38, 49, 53

balance, *balanse*, 88, 129–131, 135, 136, 140, 143

Barthes, Roland, xi, 113

Beauvoir, Simone de, 14

Becker, Ernest, 24, 125

belief (*See also* faith), 3, 5–9, 11, 12, 20, 23, 30, 102, 132

Bernard of Clairvaux, 8, 60, 61, 111, 135

birth, xii, 18, 24, 30, 35, 36, 38, 42, 50, 54, 70, 71, 73, 74–76, 81, 92, 94, 97, 108, 117, 143

body, xvii, 8, 9, 12, 14, 20, 27, 29, 31, 37, 39, 40, 42, 53, 59, 67–69, 75, 77–79, 81, 82, 91, 92, 94, 95, 98–100, 102, 105, 107, 108, 111, 112, 114–118, 120, 126, 130, 143

Brown, Karen M., 135, 136

Butler, Judith, 6, 37, 47, 48

cannibalism, 79, 92

carnival, 80, 88

castration, xix, 3, 4, 6, 10, 14–17, 19–21, 23, 43, 49, 55, 59, 81, 98, 102

Catholicism, 29, 47

chora, xii, xiv, xvi, xviii, xix, 11, 42, 44, 46, 55, 88, 91, 92, 94, 96–104, 106, 108, 115, 126, 140, 141

Christian, Christianity, xi, xvii, xviii, 8–11, 19, 20, 23, 29, 36, 39, 43, 52, 55–57, 59–63, 65, 66, 78, 79, 82, 88, 101, 112, 116, 117, 119, 121, 122, 127, 140, 142

Chrysostom, St. John, 8, 14

church, 8, 14, 33, 47, 63

circumcision, 78, 79

Cixous, Hélène, xiv, 30, 47, 123

confession(s), 11, 80, 116, 122

crucifixion, 8, 29, 33, 49

culture, xi, 5, 6, 10, 13, 17, 18, 21–23, 29, 31, 43, 47, 68–72, 80, 81, 92, 99, 100, 130

cummings, e. e., 91

dance, xv, 80, 88, 91, 135, 136, 143

Dante, 8

de Man, Paul, 31, 105

death, xiii, xvii, xix, 2, 7, 9, 12–25,

33–36, 49, 59, 61, 62, 70, 71, 75,
78–81, 87, 88, 106, 113, 114, 116, 119,
120, 125, 132, 134, 141, 143
deconstruction, 40–42, 52, 56, 91,
105, 106, 117, 141, 143
Derrida, Jacques, ix, 24, 40, 42, 46,
48, 51–53, 97, 105, 109, 117, 122
Descartes, Rene, 61, 93
desire, xi, xii, xiii, xv, xvii, xviii, 2, 4,
7, 16, 17, 19, 25, 46, 47, 58, 61, 62,
63, 65, 69–71, 74, 92–94, 97–99,
105, 107, 114–118, 122, 126, 127, 131,
141
dialogue, dialogism, xi, 31, 32, 34, 35,
38, 40, 49, 53
difference, xv, 2, 7, 11, 13, 14, 19,
21–24, 32, 33, 35, 39, 42, 51, 58, 61,
66, 73–75, 93, 94, 108, 125, 133, 135
discourse, x, xii, xiii, xv–xvii, 2, 6, 8,
9, 11–15, 19, 21–24, 29, 30, 32,
33–41, 44, 47, 49, 51, 54, 55, 57, 58,
61, 62, 63, 80, 88, 96, 97, 105, 107,
108, 111, 112, 113, 116, 117, 119, 122,
125–127, 130, 131, 133–136, 141–
143
displacement, xiii, xv, 20, 58, 70, 74,
88, 108, 109, 125
Douglas, Mary, 77
drive, xix, 4, 20, 24, 44, 49, 71, 81, 107,
135
Duns Scotus, 111, 116, 122
dyad, dyadic, xii, 1, 57–59, 64, 74, 76,
87, 108, 118, 126, 130

ecriture feminine, xiv, 10, 30, 54, 88,
113, 116, 117, 119, 120, 123, 127
ego, xiii, 45, 49, 55, 59, 93, 100, 102,
107, 119, 120
ethics (*See also* morality), xii, xviii,
xix, 9, 11, 29, 34, 45, 49, 50, 52, 60,
88, 91–96, 100–104, 107–109, 112,
121, 133, 142
Eucharist, 79, 116, 117

faith (*See also* belief), ix, xiv, 2–5, 8,

11, 12, 23, 27–29, 36, 41, 45, 52, 57,
61–63, 65, 100, 106, 122, 142
father (*See also* paternal), xiii, xv, xvi,
3–5, 8, 9, 11, 14, 18, 23, 24, 31, 42,
44, 50, 55, 58–62, 65–73, 75, 76, 78,
80–82, 92, 97, 102, 115–119, 122,
126, 127, 130, 142, 143
feminine, femininity, xiv, xv, xvii,
2–10, 13–20, 23, 30, 34, 42, 43, 44,
47–49, 51–54, 60, 65, 66, 76, 78, 87,
100, 102, 106, 111, 112, 119, 120, 123,
125, 127, 142, 143
fiction, xi, 47, 50, 88, 103, 104, 111,
126, 142–144
fictive, xi, xvii, 24, 38, 39, 56–58, 63,
65, 66, 88, 89, 91, 108, 109, 111, 127,
142, 143
fort-da game, xix, 15–18, 23
Foucault, Michel, 45, 52
Freud, 1–8, 10, 13–18, 20, 21, 23, 34,
41, 44, 49, 51, 57–59, 62, 63, 67,
69–72, 76, 81, 109, 118, 119, 122,
142, 310, 313, 315–319
*Beyond the Pleasure Principle*, 15–18,
23
*Future of an Illusion*, 3, 14, 17, 63
*Totem and Taboo*, xix, 10, 67, 71, 72,
75, 76

Gadamer, Hans-Georg, 66
Galileo, 61
Gallop, Jane, 19, 38, 43, 44, 47, 51
gender, xiv, xv, 2, 4–6, 13–16, 19,
21–23, 35, 52, 65–69, 76, 77, 81, 87,
88, 118, 119, 123, 141, 142
Girard, René, 1, 2, 66–77, 80, 81, 87,
88
goddess, 9, 16, 82, 102
Grosz, Elizabeth, 44, 47, 50–52

Hegel, G. W. F., 34, 94–96, 104, 109
Heidegger, Martin, 104, 109
herethics, 9, 29, 34, 36
hermeneutic(s), 10, 65, 66, 68, 112, 140

heterogeneity, xii, xiii, 31, 32, 51, 79, 93–95, 97, 100–102, 109, 116, 126, 130, 139

identification, xv, xix, 9, 25, 33, 34, 39, 52, 53, 57, 58, 62, 70, 71, 73–75, 102, 104, 118, 122, 131, 141, 142
illusion, xvii, xix, 3–5, 7, 12, 14, 17, 23, 24, 37, 57, 62, 63, 103, 125, 139, 142–144
imaginary, xii, xiii, xv, xix, 20, 25, 30, 31, 33, 55, 56, 58–63, 73, 75, 81, 82, 89, 94, 107, 108, 127
imagination, xvii, 20, 31, 88, 93, 101, 103, 111, 114, 115, 116, 126, 143
incarnation, 12, 40, 117
incest, 71, 72, 76, 78, 81, 99, 123
intertext, intertextuality, 31, 48, 49, 53, 93, 106, 125
Irigaray, Luce, 1, 30, 47, 67, 68, 73, 80, 123

Jardine, Alice, 1, 13, 44, 46, 48
Johnson, Barbara, 48
Jones, Ann Rosalind, 28, 47
jouissance, 6, 12, 33, 44, 52, 79, 88, 92, 101, 102, 125, 129, 131–137, 139
joy, 12, 88, 102, 116, 129–137, 139, 140

Kant, Immanuel, 93, 104
Kierkegaard, Soren, 102, 109
Klein, Melanie, 98
Kristeva, Julia (biographical), ix–xii, xiv, 27–28, 40, 47, 49
  *Black Sun*, xii, xiv, xviii, 7, 19, 23
  *Desire in Language*, xi, xii, xviii, 7, 46, 47, 92–94, 99, 105
  Étrangers a nous-mêmes, xiv, xvi, xviii, 34
  *In the Beginning Was Love*, xiv, 7–9, 11, 12, 23, 29, 41, 44, 45, 47, 49, 52, 61, 100, 120, 122, 142
  *Powers of Horror*, xiv, xvi, xviii, 2, 3, 7–9, 12, 23, 24, 42, 49, 51, 67, 82, 92, 99–101, 111, 122, 132

*Revolution in Poetic Language*, xii, xviii, 31, 34, 44, 48, 54, 91, 92, 94–98, 105, 106, 121, 134
  "Stabat Mater," xii, xiv, xv, xvii, xviii, 7–9, 11, 12, 19, 23, 24, 27–34, 36, 38, 40, 42–44, 46, 48, 50, 53–56, 141
  *Tales of Love*, xiv, xviii, 2, 3, 7, 25, 57, 59, 60, 67, 82, 106, 111, 114, 121–123, 132, 142
  "Women's Time," xv, xviii, 1, 7, 8, 10, 12, 23, 30, 37, 102, 121, 133

Lacan, x–xix, 1, 2, 5–8, 11, 13, 15, 16, 18, 19, 23, 24, 27, 31, 39, 40, 42, 43, 48, 49, 51, 54, 55, 57, 58, 59, 73, 74, 92, 93, 97, 98, 106, 107, 109, 118, 122, 127, 130
lack, 2, 9, 14–16, 18, 19, 22, 33, 36, 42, 58, 68, 81, 122, 131
language, x–xix, 6–8, 10–12, 15, 18, 19, 21, 23, 27, 30, 31, 32, 34, 36, 40–49, 51, 54, 55, 58, 68, 69, 70–75, 77, 78, 91–94, 97–100, 105, 111, 112, 113, 115–117, 120, 121, 125, 126, 129, 130, 131, 133–135, 142, 143
Lautréamont, Comte de, 134
law, 37, 59, 71, 81, 92, 96, 112, 115–119, 126, 130, 131, 139, 140, 143
Law of the Father (*See also* Name of the Father), xiii, xv, 23, 58, 80, 82, 92, 97, 102, 115, 116, 118, 119, 122, 143
Lévi-Strauss, Claude, 311
linguistic(s), xiii, xv, 6, 8, 19, 28, 30–32, 35, 40, 41, 55, 69, 70, 77, 80, 81, 96, 98, 100, 105, 106, 109, 111, 115, 121
Logos, 4, 36, 39, 97
love, 11, 12, 17, 28, 29, 32–34, 36, 39, 41, 46–47, 52, 57–62, 65, 66, 74, 75, 82, 89, 100, 112, 118, 122

MacIntyre, Alasdair, 104
Mallarmé, Stéphane, 30, 48, 134

Marx, Marxism, xii, 28, 32, 94–96, 109
Mary (Virgin), 8, 9, 19, 23, 24, 29, 33–35, 39, 49, 52, 77, 111
masculine, xv, xvi, 3, 4, 14, 15, 17, 43, 44, 118, 119, 127
mastery, xv, 20, 27, 37, 39, 55, 56, 133, 136, 139, 143
matricide, 20, 21
melancholia (See also Kristeva, Black Sun), 20
Merleau-Ponty, Maurice, 104, 109
metaphor, 1, 3, 18, 19, 23, 27, 29, 34, 40–43, 45, 46, 47, 50–56, 58, 97, 105, 127, 141, 142
Mill, John Stuart, 104
mimesis, mimicry, xvi, 58, 69–75, 81, 88, 121
mirror, 2, 56, 98, 310, 312, 313
misogyny, 2, 7, 15, 18, 21, 22
model, 23, 24, 33, 38, 53, 55, 65, 69, 70, 73, 74, 82, 129, 136, 142
Moi, Toril, 44–48, 105, 120
morality (See also ethics), 3, 4, 9, 13, 34, 63, 78, 91–93, 96, 100, 101, 103, 104, 107, 134, 143
mother, xii–xvii, 2–12, 15–21, 23–25, 27–30, 32–35, 38–44, 46, 50, 53, 55–60, 62, 66, 67, 69, 70, 72, 73, 75–82, 87, 92, 94, 98, 102, 108, 115, 118, 119, 127, 130, 141, 142
murder, 67–72, 75–77, 79
music, 9, 36, 50, 113, 131
mysticism, 3, 6, 63, 135, 136
myth, xv, 1, 9, 16, 33, 34, 39, 42, 59, 60, 67, 68, 70, 76, 78, 97, 102, 105, 143

Name of the Father (See also Law of the Father), xii, 55, 130
narcissism, xiv, xvi–xx, 1, 10, 33, 34, 43, 49, 57–67, 73–75, 77, 81, 87, 92, 95, 107–109, 112, 118, 141, 142
narrative, xi, 16, 27, 29, 30, 35, 36, 39, 40, 50, 55, 79, 100, 101, 104
Nietzsche, Friedrich, 41, 42, 50, 109
nothing, nothingness, 1, 6, 13–15, 20, 25, 34, 57, 58, 61, 63, 66, 72, 95, 97, 103, 104, 115, 134, 141
novel, x–xii, 31, 38, 48

object relations, 4–6
Oedipus complex, Oedipal stage, xiv–xvi, 3–5, 44, 49, 54, 57, 58, 69–73, 76, 81, 82, 98, 106
Ong, Walter, 50
other, x–xvii, 1, 5, 6, 8, 13, 19, 22–25, 29, 41, 42, 49, 53–63, 69–82, 92, 97, 107, 108, 115, 117, 118, 120, 122, 127, 132, 142, 143

paternal (See also father), xiii, xv–xvii, 2, 5, 9, 11, 15, 17, 21, 34, 37, 38, 41, 51, 52, 54, 60, 73, 74, 89
patriarchy, -al, xvi, 11, 23, 37, 59, 60, 66, 69, 77, 82, 87, 97, 101, 102, 108, 119
patricide, 71, 72
Peirce, Charles S., 118, 122
penis envy, 14
phallus, phallic, phallocentrism, xv, xvii, 6, 15, 19, 20, 21, 42–44, 51, 54, 55, 58–60, 65, 74, 127, 142, 143
Plato, xii, 11, 44, 96, 97, 105, 115
Plotinus, 59
politics, xii, xv, xvi, 10, 28, 45–47, 49, 102, 105, 141
pollution, 8, 78, 81, 82
postmodernism, 28, 30, 40, 48, 91–94, 100–103, 112, 120
practice, 31, 34, 45, 50, 52, 54, 63, 65, 88, 92, 93–97, 100–102, 104, 107–109, 113, 118, 120, 122, 125, 133, 136, 139, 142
praxis, 95, 96, 104, 109
prayer, 65, 88, 119, 120, 139, 143, 318
prehistory (individual), xvi, 44, 55, 66, 71, 73, 75, 82, 118, 127, 142

presence, xvi, 13–19, 21–24, 54, 57, 74, 126, 130
prière féminine, 65, 111, 119, 123, 127
prohibition, 71, 72, 76–78, 81
purification, purity, 10, 12, 77, 78, 81, 108

Rawls, John, 104
reading, xvii, xix, 27, 29, 32, 38, 39, 48, 53, 55, 56
real, xiii, 5–7, 12, 31, 38, 41, 43, 47, 53, 71, 96–98, 108, 111, 113, 116, 119–122, 126, 127, 141, 143
receptacle, 9, 11, 36, 44, 52, 97, 98, 105
renunciation, 2–4, 13, 14, 15, 17, 23, 52
resurrection, 49, 59
Ricoeur, Paul, 105
rite, 68, 77, 78
Roudiez, Leon S., ix, 2, 46, 47, 106, 120–122

sacred, 1, 2, 9, 10, 23, 24, 51, 67, 69, 70, 72, 76, 80–82, 87, 100, 121, 132
sacrifice, 33, 52, 67–73, 75–77, 80, 81, 87–89, 108, 139, 143
Sade, Marquis de, 61
Saussure, Ferdinand de, xiii
scapegoat, 1, 70, 75, 81, 88
Schrag, Calvin, 109
Scotus (See Duns Scotus)
self-division, 55, 88, 125, 129, 131–134, 136, 137, 139, 140
semiotics, semiology, xii, xiv–xvi, 30, 35, 63, 125, 127, 142, 143
signification, xiii, 19, 43, 51, 54, 55, 88, 96, 97, 100, 107–109, 130, 143
signified, xiii, 33, 40, 54, 93, 107
signifier, xiii, 19, 40, 43, 51, 54, 70, 72, 97, 107, 126
signifying practice, xix, 88, 92, 94, 97, 102, 104, 107, 108, 109, 125, 142
sin, 9, 10, 66, 77, 79, 80, 116, 117, 122, 126

Smith, Paul, 1, 28, 37, 46, 47
Sollers, Philippe, xi, 28, 44, 48
soul, 6, 7, 18, 111, 112, 114, 115, 119, 126
sound, 36, 54, 113, 120, 130
split, splitting, xvii, xviii, xx, 7–9, 27, 29, 32, 33, 38–40, 42, 45, 54, 55, 74, 88, 98–100, 101, 106, 121, 132
Stanton, Domna, 42–44, 47, 51, 55
Stevens, Wallace, 103, 104, 106, 108
sublimation, xvi, xvii, xix, 43, 51, 57, 59, 60, 132
substitute, substitution, xiii, xv, 23, 51, 58, 67–70, 73, 81, 88, 118
superego, 3, 4, 34, 98, 102

Taylor, Mark C., 10, 18, 24
Tel Quel, xi, 29, 48
Tertullian, 14
text, xii, 31, 35, 38–40, 48–50, 53–56, 87, 93, 97, 105, 106, 139
theology, xvii, 8–10, 24, 41, 51, 74, 82, 91, 107, 108, 111–113, 116, 117, 119–122, 125–127, 143
third party, triad, xv–xvii, 57–61, 63, 64, 70, 73 75, 87, 88, 126, 127, 142
Thomas Aquinas, 60, 61, 88, 111–118, 121, 126, 135
time, 10, 50, 95, 103
Todorov, Tzvetan, ix–xi
transference, xii, xix, 11, 12, 23, 61, 118, 122, 127, 143
transformation, x, 11, 14, 23, 32, 45, 96
transgression, 29, 32, 37, 42, 45, 46, 54, 55, 116
transitional objects, 17, 18

unconscious, x, 1, 3, 18, 19, 31, 34, 38, 39, 45, 62, 63, 93, 97, 107, 109
unity (of self or subject), xiii, xiv, 1, 6, 9, 19, 38, 45, 74, 93–96, 98, 101, 103, 107, 108, 126, 131

Valery, Paul, 48
Van Herik, Judith, 4, 13, 14, 17, 21–23
victim, 60, 67, 69, 70, 72, 77, 81
violence, xvii–xix, 1, 2, 49, 63, 65,
    67–77, 80, 81, 87, 88, 108, 116, 132,
    133, 143
Virgin Mary (*See* Mary)
Vodou, 135, 136, 140
vréel, 113, 117, 120, 121, 126

Walzer, Michael, 104
Winnicott, D. W., 1, 2, 4, 5, 7, 12, 15,
    17, 18, 23
Winquist, Charles, 18, 122, 127
wish, 3, 7, 12, 14, 16, 66, 123
writing, 32, 48, 50, 113
Wyschogrod, Edith, 123, 127

zero degree of subjectivity, 25, 57, 74

- Virginia Bunos
- Ant Pressly -

in Christology - If we see the
birth are attached to the mother
will we see the x

X-ant had the opportunity to see
his mother as divine. The early
mother In fact devoxed him -
made her ideal of woman what
no woman can meet -

J. as teenager